David G
Grade 3

the tragi**comic** memoir
of a reluctant atheist

BOOK ONE

David Robert Loblaw
(formerly David G)

Cameron House Media

DavidGGrade3.com

Loblaw, David Robert, author
David G Grade 3: the tragicomic memoir of a reluctant atheist

Memoir
Humour

Issued in print, electronic, and audio formats
ISBN 978-0-9959495-0-8 (print book)
ISBN 978-0-9959495-1-5 (electronic book)
ISBN 978-0-9959495-2-2 (audio book)

Inquiries:
See contact info at DavidGGrade3.com

Cameron House Media

For the two women who created me.
My mom and my sister.

PART THREE:
CHURCH

PART FOUR:
HOME

PART FIVE: DEATH

PART SIX: HEAVEN

Prologue: Two Truths

Wild with excitement, I race into my house, slam my baseball mitt on the kitchen table, screaming: "When I grow up, I'm gonna be a BASEBALL player!"

My mom stops what she is doing and slowly turns to me.

"David, the closest you'll ever get to professional baseball," she says, "is to get Lou Gehrig's Disease."

My mother never said this. My sister insists she did.

Herein lies the quintessential struggle in writing every part of this book. I have many childhood memories, all covered in my uncertainty on how the stories have been tainted with either my staid mother's depressing negativity or my flamboyant big sister's funny flair.

"It's not a lie if it makes a good story," I hear from my sister.

"Telling a lie is a venial sin," I hear from my mom.

These are the two women who raise me. Each having one of my arms, pulling in opposite directions. Dumb David in the middle with exactly 50/50 divided loyalties. Go with my blasphemous big sister and have a scary fun time ... or ... stay with my brooding, tortured mother and have all the comforts of a safe childhood home.

Decades later, while I am preparing the dual funeral of my mom and sister, the pissy priest is giving me a strict two-minute time limit for each eulogy. He is a traditional priest who dislikes eulogies usurping his Funeral Mass, reluctantly allowing a lay person to speak before the service starts.

After accepting my word of having the Catholic sacraments of Baptism, Communion, Confession, and Confirmation, he allows me to go up to his pulpit in his church to summarize their lives in a few words before the official start of the Mass I've paid for.

As I never got a chance to properly brag about these two loving and loyal women—each in their own way—this book is my attempt to fully flesh out their lives. And mine too.

The first part of this book describes the eight main characters in my childhood, one of which I never meet. The next sections are School, Church, Home, Death, and finally, Heaven. The first chapters, especially about my mom's early life, may seem a bit grim and damn depressing, but it does get funnier later on. Much funnier — I promise.

Though I do not use full family names for any of the people in these stories, I do use their real first names or nicknames and all are real individual people — some living, most dead.

All of the locations are real.

Every story is true in all that I know, have been told, have eavesdropped, or have researched.

All dialogue is, of course, a reconstruction from memory as my mom was too cheap to buy me the spy microphone that I wanted.

I was known as David G for the first 22 years of my life. In 1982, I legally changed my name to my current one. As you read my memoir, it won't take you long before you understand why I severed my birth name.

To see photos of many of the characters and locations in this book, go to my book website, DavidGGrade3.com.

A note to those listening to this on audio-book: I apologize in advance for my verbal mangling of every one of the non-English words and phrases in French, Cree, and spoken Latin.

I have researched and practised as much as I can, but this brings back painful and humiliating memories of my trip to China in 1989. I had a phrase book that I studied diligently for months beforehand, though every time I had the confidence to speak while in China, everyone's eyes would pop open and tilt to the top of my head.

I was convinced that no matter what I said, no matter what intonation, it always sounded like: "Hello, my hat is on fire."

David Robert Loblaw
(formerly David G)
anno Domini 2018

PART ONE: CHARACTERS

Chapter 1: My Mother's Parents

Like a perfect Catholic, my maternal grandmother gives birth to her first child nine months after her wedding night. She and my grandfather were hoping for a boy, but a first-born girl is okay.

One year later, in 1929, another birth and another girl. A year later, 1930, yet another girl. ("We need that boy to take over the farm in the future.") The next year, 1931, sees my mother, Irene, born. ("Why is God not giving us a boy?") One more year, 1932, and one more girl.

Five annual babies, all healthy, but all female. All I can imagine is the sound my farmer grandfather must make upon hearing each year's bad birth news.

It then takes God a few years to decide that the time is right and a boy is finally given to the world in 1935.

Though blessed with a quick succession of five girls and a strong boy, my grandmother's childbearing duties are ended in great shame and public humiliation eleven years later when their oopsie baby girl is born. They got their boy; why did they ever engage in the filthy act one more time after all these years?

Chapter 2: My Mother, Irene

It is early winter 1950 on the frozen Saskatchewan prairies and the Priest is bundling up for the cold walk from his rectory to a certain house in town.

Having the Priest visit your home is one of the greatest blessings a devout Catholic family can receive. After receiving word the Priest has accepted the invitation, there is a frenzy of cooking and cleaning throughout the house. The blessed family will soon have *In persona Christi capitis* sitting right there at the kitchen table, eating the farm family's beef and potatoes and carrots. A highlight of the year, if not the decade.

The knock on the door is heard by everyone. Looking out, they are horrified the Priest is standing on the front step. Why is he here? They were never informed he had accepted the invitation. There is nothing prepared. The family is ruined; the farm is lost. No number of rosaries and penance will be able to erase their sin and avoid the family's eviction from church life. The parents, their five teen daughters, one son, and baby girl will soon be homeless beggars on the Protestant side of town.

With desperate intensity, they pray the Priest is not here for an expected supper but maybe, hopefully, is just delivering terrible news.

The crying girls are sent away to the farthest room. The young boy slips away and hides by the front door where the parents await their fate.

Though the boy cannot see the Priest or his parents, he can

easily eavesdrop and is confused as it seems the Priest is asking for one of the boy's sisters. He hears footsteps, then murmurs, then loud sobs from the back room. More footsteps back to the front door.

It makes no sense to him whatsoever but it sounds like one of his big sisters is being asked if she is with child.

Standing in front of her parents and the Priest, eighteen-year-old Irene is more shocked than she will ever be in her life and cannot speak. She is so scared and confused. There is no way in the world the Priest can know she is pregnant; she confessed her sin in Confession so only God knows.

The Priest, with his heavenly compassion, offers the mother of the family two choices. She and her soiled daughter can quietly leave the community forever or the soiled daughter can quietly leave the community forever. Irene's mother chooses the second option, and starts to arrange her daughter's ostracism.

On her nineteenth birthday in April 1950, Irene, five months pregnant, makes the worst mistake of her entire life, though sadly she has no choice.

Far away from her family farm community, in a farce of the Roman Catholic sacrament of marriage, she becomes the wife of someone she barely knows: the violent drunk known as Maurice-the-piece-of-shit. Their arranged wedding is in Moose Jaw, a big city 130 miles away, a place where she has no family or friends. (I have yet to discover why my mother's mother chose that place.) Irene's only wedding present is the presence of one family member: her big sister Anna, who has a teaching position in a nearby town. No other family member was allowed to attend.

What makes all of this surprising is teen Irene was always known as Miss Goody Two Shoes, the perfect daughter. Before this, whenever any of her four sisters got in trouble for anything, they would receive a severe scolding from Mother, demanding the reason why they cannot be like Perfect Irene.

She had been escalated to Family Sainthood a few years earlier in 1947 when strong and healthy Father was suddenly sickened —bedridden by something unknown— and she piously accepts stopping her high school education at age sixteen to help run the farm. Her four other teen sisters silently nod their heads.

Two years later, as quickly as it appeared, Irene's father's mysterious illness disappears and he returns to run the farm at full strength. He never again has any other health issue in his long life of ninety-two years, aside from deafness at the end.

Suddenly alone and directionless, teen Irene has nothing to look forward to — her sisters ahead of her in education, her friends having left her behind.

After my mother's death, I find a letter in her hand-writing. She describes how, at age eighteen, she meets the carefree young man who will ruin her life forever. It is not addressed to anyone.

I met Maurice at a country school dance. Feeling trapped at home, I marvelled at the freedom he had. He was not responsible to anyone and never had any rules to live by. Most of the time he would drink too heavily. My parents never drank so little did I know then of the consequences.

Sex education being taboo in the home, meant I was very ill informed*. I soon found out that I was pregnant. I couldn't tell my parents at the time. Two months later I was operated for appendicitis (hoping that I would lose the baby.)

Mother found out and arranged for me to leave and go to Moose Jaw where we would get married. Being brainwashed that all Catholics had to get married, that left me no way out. Mother didn't want us to get married in our home town as that would be a disgrace being pregnant.

[* When I show this letter to one of my mom's sisters, she laughs at the part of not being informed about sex education. "Oh c'mon, we were farm kids! We knew exactly what did what."]

Though only eight of Irene's seventy-eight years of life merge with that stranger she marries on her nineteenth birthday, the events during those few years fully define and fully destroy her entire life. The three children they have together will be her life's focus, especially the first born.

Chapter 3: My Oldest Brother, Louis

Though conceived out-of-wedlock, Irene's first-born is not considered a bastard as she and the father are legally married when Louis is born in August 1950. (You'll later find out I am the bastard of the family, born exactly ten years later.)

Louis is the perfect child: well-mannered, smart, polite, kind, soft-spoken, gentle. He is tall and thin like me, but with curious green eyes and bright red hair inherited from his never-seen paternal grandfather, Big Red — a giant, angry man who could pound back a beer with one hand while pounding a head with the other. To see her son so untainted by the vile violent bloodline of his father is the only thing that keeps Irene going.

Louis disappears for hours, only to be discovered in his hiding places filled with books. My sister brags of her big brother's straight As in every subject in all eight years at St. Augustine School. He becomes an altar boy at Little Flower Church. Louis goes on to Campion Catholic High School where he continues to excel in all subjects, especially Latin, and starts on a path to becoming a master chess player.

On to his first year in the Engineering faculty at the Regina Campus of the University of Saskatchewan where afterwards he takes a summer break to go to the West Coast in 1970 at age twenty.

From a letter written by Louis to our mother:
> I just happened to be around when LSD was used in an intellectual way and heroin was so

plentiful in the early 70's you couldn't hardly help but get addicted.

Louis is dead three days before being discovered, his oxygen tank continuing to breath air into his lifeless lungs. It is now 2004 and he has been a drug addict in downtown Vancouver for over thirty years.

He is always a kind, distant uncle to me — never really feeling like brothers. I am three years old, maybe four, sitting in my little grey rocking chair watching The Friendly Giant on CBC Television. I pop alive for this incredible show shot in an enormous castle featuring a giant, a rooster, and a giraffe. The giant's name is Friendly; Rusty is the harp-playing rooster in a book-filled sack nailed to the wall; and Jerome is a giraffe who sticks his head into the medieval castle window.

Each episode ends when the giant, the first male figure in my life, puts away the miniature furniture, the castle's drawbridge is raised, and — my favourite part — a cow jumps over the moon at the end. During one episode I hear Louis behind me say, "The cow's not gonna make it over the moon today."

I burst into tears and become hysterical.

My big brother sits down on the rug beside me, trying to talk me down from my crisis, saying he was just kidding. Together we watch the rest of the show, with its successful cow jumping conclusion.

This is the first memory of my life.

I write the eulogy of Louis and read it out loud at his service in front of our mom, some of her friends, a few family, and none of his friends, ending it with:

> When we cleared out his Vancouver apartment last week, we found books everywhere — on the couch, on his bed, on the fridge, on every counter and shelf. As we piled up the books to ready them to be given away, I noticed the staggering range of his interests: classic literature and modern paperbacks; books on economics, biology, art, world cultures; several Bibles, books on the Buddha; computer manuals.
>
> And that's the paradox of Louis.
>
> He was insatiably interested in all areas of human experience, yet chose to be an outside observer, never participating.
>
> A beautiful mind. A mystery to all.

I feel bad concentrating on the latter part of my big brother's life, the druggie part, but it is a huge part — two-thirds, in fact. From his birth to age 20, Louis is smart, polite, perfect. From ages 20 to 54, he is alcoholic, drug addict, dead.

And I know he is the most profound disappointment to a mother I can ever imagine.

Children always half-jokingly pester their parents on who is their favourite. To maintain household peace, most never say and most treat every child the same as the others. My mother is fanatical about doing this, though we all know who her favourite is. Throughout our lives, my sister and I constantly compete for Second Place in Mom's eyes, easily conceding top spot to Louis.

After burying her son, Irene builds a shrine to him in her bedroom. When her daughter, my big sister, dies a few years later, there is no shrine for her. I always wonder if I had died before my mother if she would have built one for me. I hope so — the Shrine to St. Louis is beautiful. My mother sure has a knack for that.

Chapter 4: My Little Big Sister, Yvette

Though biologically correct because we have different fathers, I hate calling my sister my half-sister.

She is everything to me. She does as much as my mother in raising me; she is the closest blood family I have ever known. Without her wild sense of humour and support through my bad-skin teen years—with comforting words like "You have to smile more, you have the face of a purse snatcher"—it is unlikely I would have made it into adulthood.

Louis is only fifteen months old when she appears as his Christmas present in 1951. They have an instant lifelong bond: her playfulness a perfect antidote to his seriousness. And so

9

different in personality and in appearance: he, tall, red-hair, translucent skin, serious; she, short, black hair, olive skin, laughing.

As their father is always "between jobs," meaning he was again fired for being drunk and probably violent, they move a lot in the early 1950s — with the two kids and mother only having each other for stability.

Louis is born in Moose Jaw, Saskatchewan; his sister in Castor, Alberta; no family connection in either. Always on the move throughout Western Canada, the next stop is always where their father will make it big.

After as many moves as diaper changes, Irene, the twenty-one-year-old mother and wife of an angry drunk, finds herself in Vancouver with a toddler and a baby. While Maurice looks for suitable work, sometimes disappearing for days, Irene gets a part-time job at the Vancouver General Hospital as a cleaner, reluctantly leaving her children for a few hours each day with a kind elderly neighbour who comes over to their rented room.

During one cleaning shift at the hospital, Irene is told to leave immediately and to go to Emergency as her neighbours are rushing in her daughter.

Maurice had stumbled home, became verbally violent with the babysitter, making Louis cower in the corner, his baby sister scream in her crib.

Suddenly, it's completely silent.

The babysitter runs from the room.

There is hysteria out in the hallways of the rooming house.

A half dozen people force themselves in the room and scream at Maurice: "What the hell have you done?"

Women swoop down to the silent baby in the crib, flopped over against the back wooden railing. The men tell Maurice if they see him again, they'll kill him.

Irene spends the next several weeks bedside in the hospital with her baby girl recovering from a head injury and in the same hospital cleaning toilets, going home to be with her terrified toddler boy.

My mom's writing:

> There were many moves during the three years we were in Vancouver. I worked for about a year. One of the worst experience was when he injured our year old daughter. She was in the hospital for over a week for observation due to head injuries. I laid charges. He was put in jail, but a Social Worker for the A.A. helped him. He went north to work on the Radar DEW Line in the Northwest Territories.

In a letter from Louis to our mother:

> What he did to Yvette was so inexcusable, it has to be psychopathic behaviour. Can you imagine someone hurting their own daughter when a baby simply because of crying?

After saving some money, selling all their furniture, and

11

somehow getting a secret cash donation from her own father, Irene carries her two children onto a train back to the flat prairies.

In the 1980s, living in a mountainous small city near Vancouver, Yvette makes meals for her two girls and husband, but also makes a fifth serving to be set aside for her big brother. These extra servings are frozen in small containers and are brought to Louis en masse once a month or whenever next they make a quick side trip to Downtown Eastside Vancouver.

These are so often and commonly referred to as "louie-containers" the little girls assume that is the regular name for every family's leftover containers, which leads to an embarrassing realization many years later amongst their friends at school.

In my mother's papers that I go through after her death, I find this in a letter written by my brother Louis,

> My sister and I were always close. We fought a lot when we were children, but she always maintained close contact with me and made me a part of her life even though I was in a totally different society class.
>
> I remember once when she asked me to come at X-mas (as she always did) and I said to her "Yvette, X-mas is for your family, I feel uncomfortable being there," and she said to me "Louis, you are my family." I never forgot that.

In a letter to Yvette written in the mid-1980s, Mom writes,
> As a child you could always express your feelings outwardly. You made me angry many times with your outbursts but at least you got it out of your system. On the contrary, Louis never expressed himself, but he took refuge under drugs.

For me, the youngest child, my big sister is my mentor, the keeper of my secrets, the creator of all things funny. I first learn the true nature of family, friends, of life itself from her biting characterizations. Her tongue a hilarious moral machete, she leaves me in stitches every time in nearly thirty years of live performances.

I am ten when she becomes a nurse and moves far away from me. Her daily live commentaries dwindle to monthly letters and occasional collect phone calls — all hilarious, but not the same. From then on, I only catch her shows once or twice a year at Christmas or mid-summer. She is the most lively, funny, talented, theatrical person I have ever known never to think about going into show business.

My sister thrills and chills me at the same time: the perfect dramatic combination. Every time she mimics a nun or a relative or a political figure, I laugh with a tight fear. Her clinical dissection of people is an art form. I giggle and cringe simultaneously, knowing we are in so much trouble if Sister Margaret or Gramma or U.S. President Nixon find out we are making fun of them. I'm so scared for her and me if we're caught. She does not seem the least bit concerned.

But it's her thievery that scares me for her soul. She laughs it off as admitting she is "just a klepto." Her teen bedroom is filled with objects collected from all around the city: street signs; lawn ornaments; a beautiful metal candle frame with a marble base stolen from a fine dining restaurant, probably L'Habitant. There is a flashing yellow light coming from her bedroom — I have a closer look and she has stolen a city construction barricade.

Yvette and I are at Kresge's department store downtown on 11th looking for a Mother's Day greeting card. After many choices, we decide on one. With it held high, in full view of everyone, she walks out of the store — me right beside, her unknowing accomplice. On the sidewalk, realizing what just happened, I am scared shitless knowing we are going to jail and then to Hell.

"Don't worry," she says. "If they catch us, I'll start crying and say I was day-dreaming, didn't know what I was doing." That is her modus operandi and it always works. And she knows the weapons she possesses: cute, small, thoroughly innocent. I know my sister is guilty but I tell no one until now.

It is 2007 and I am sitting in the stuffy office at the funeral company making final arrangements for my mom's and sister's funeral a few weeks hence. Mom has brilliantly pre-planned and pre-paid everything — except what is to be etched in each

14

urn.

The sweaty salesman is staring at me, waiting behind his desk, pen in hand, to write the maximum of three lines, fifty characters total, including spaces and punctuation. It has to be sent to the engraver this afternoon if it is going to ready in time.

I recite my mother's bare biographical details of full name, birth date, death date, and that's about it. The salesman writes it down.

For my sister I want something more poetic, more vibrant, one with pizazz:

1951 to 2006

~ a liar and a thief ~

The salesman stops writing and looks up at me with the dumbest look in his face.

"That ain't happening," he says.

I says it's an in-joke, a whole family story behind it, something she would think was hilarious.

"It ain't happening."

Looking back at it now, I should have insisted. I am the customer and this is what I want. Instead, her urn buried in prairie dirt reads:

1951 to 2006

~ a storyteller and a collector ~

My sister has a charismatic warmth that brings you in, an entertaining flamboyance. It is exhilarating being on her good side, which I always am.

15

But there is one thing that sadly taints our relationship throughout our lives: her lifelong and inexplicable reluctance to destroy our brother, Ape.

Chapter 5: My Half-brother, Half-ape

After Maurice's quick escape from Vancouver, Irene does not see her deadbeat drunk of a husband for several years. This difficult but violence-free time from Maurice is broken one day when he suddenly walks in the front door of her new home in Saskatchewan in late 1955.

And when he shows up, no matter what he has said and done in the past, she cannot refuse him entry to her new home and bed as he is still her legally-married husband. It is a heart-wrenching reality that a battered woman in the 1950s has no societal recourse but to open her family's front door to a known violent man who has hospitalized her baby in a drunken rage.

Soon after Maurice's out-of-the-blue return, my mother's third child is conceived. Though no fault of his own, of course, this second boy, my half-brother Ape, is a dead ringer for his father.

I will never know the circumstances surrounding his conception roughly on Valentine's Day 1956, but I'm guessing it was not littered with freshly-cut roses (my mother's middle name), a sensual body oil massage to squeeze out the tensions

16

of working seven days a week, or a properly chilled Pinot Grigio, though alcohol is most likely involved.

His third child still in diapers, Maurice walks out the door and abandons his family, his stench forever permeating Irene and their three children — and seeping onto me, born years later without any genetic connection.

Her words in a letter I find:

> Due to the constant mental and physical pressures, I knew that I was slowly falling closer to the Mental Institution or the grave. My father realized the conditions and gave me the $300 for a Legal Separation. Maurice was forced to leave so he went back up north and I haven't seen him since.

The source of Ape's nickname is our sister's vibrant imagination. She claims he was the world's hairiest baby, never losing his fur as he ages. Ape is shaving before he leaves elementary school; he is the tall one in the back of his Grade Eight class photo, the one with the Fred Flintstone five o'clock shadow.

I hate those sappy stories and Norman Rockwell paintings of little boys looking up at their father or older brothers in front of the bathroom mirror, mimicking their shaving, wishing time would speed up so they too could be part of this masculine ritual. Looking at my big brother, I am terrified of my future: I do not want to grow up if I have to shave my entire face several times a day.

And Ape is hairy all over, especially on his back. Yvette

17

jokes that we should dye him green, vaseline his back hair into points, and make him run around the neighbourhood as Godzilla.

My oldest brother Louis and I are built small, thin, mild-mannered; Ape is big, muscular, and hostile. My sister says Mom just had him so she would have someone around to move furniture.

Everyone in our school and neighbourhood knows Ape. Every store owner tenses when he enters. Every parent wonders how Irene deals with him. We all wonder when he will do something extremely bad, so bad he'll be finally taken away and our mother's name will be all over The Leader-Post.

The cycle of Ape getting riled up, getting in trouble, getting caught, being punished is relentless for our mother. I am an expert at tuning out all of Ape's escapades, the same way I do when my hippy-dippy teen siblings go on and on about that silly-sounding place called "Nam." I love being in my own little world and I strive to stay in it by myself as much as possible. But, of course, Ape's world often collides with mine.

He breaks open my locked suitcase under my bed, smashes open the plastic display trays for my coin collection, steals every sequential penny, nickel, dime, and quarter from 1930 to 1966, plus the full 1967 Centennial coin collection.

He is staring at me from his place across the table during suppertime, a smug grin on his face. I look down to my mineral collection Mom allows me to keep by my plate and see one rock missing. I look back at Ape and he's pointing to his open

18

mouth.

There is always a valid reason for everyone's nickname in our neighbourhood. Ape is hairy. Hippo is fat. Hamster is tiny. Mute never talks. Brian the Brain is smart. Fem is a slightly feminine boy. Flake has a severe dry skin problem. Gotch's underwear is always showing. Patsy the Flea supposedly has fleas. Mouldy Susan has a facial skin disorder which requires cream with a greenish tinge. And Mean Dean is simply mean.

I want a nickname too, a cool one, but I never get one. All I have ever been known as is Ape's Little Brother and I don't like that at all. I'm too dim to realize it at the time, but that is not a nickname. It's a warning.

I am a scrawny little kid in a tough neighbourhood filled with bullies and beatings. Each morning, I leave my home in the Greer Court projects and start my walk to school by myself, wearing my shiny-black orthopaedic Oxford shoes, carrying my brown leather schoolbag filled with my NASA documents in one hand, a microscope or rocket in the other. It always takes me a long time to get to school as I love stopping to watch some loser get pushed and kicked around by Mean Dean or another school bully.

"Oooo you're gonna be in trouble with Sister," I mutter to the sobbing, bleeding kid on his hands and knees, picking up crumbled school papers scattered on the sidewalk, then continue on my way.

It is not until I am an adult do I realize I lived my childhood in an invisible protective bubble. Though I never see Ape actually step in to defend me, no bully ever bothers me, not even once. It seems everyone but me knew the secret code of, "Touch David, and Ape will smash your face in."

Even if I had been bright enough to know why I was the only nerd never picked on, I still would not have thanked my brother. We never get along. Though our ages are only four years apart and we sleep in bunkbeds in the same bedroom, we lead completely separate childhoods. I have no memory of playing any type of game together.

The only one-on-one interaction I recall is when he tries to teach me how to ride his bike. He places me on the seat, my toes barely touching the pedals, and he starts running alongside, holding the back of the seat, until he gives a big push and releases me. I'm rolling down the lawn, terrified, not knowing how to stop. The front wheel starts wobbling, and I hit the ground hard, face in the grass.

"Fucken goof! Bent the spokes!" he yells, lifts the bike off me, and rides away.

I limp back to the house, angry as hell, to go cry in secret. As I start up the stairs, I pass by his and my Hilroy school notebooks we keep on either side of the landing. I pick up all of his and take them upstairs. At my bedroom desk, I push aside my important research papers, grab a thick black felt pen, pick up each one of his notebooks, and write in big block letters on every cover:

20

APE IS MENTAL
APE IS MENTAL
APE IS MENTAL

I place them back on the landing, then hide under my bed, waiting for Mom to punish me. But she never arrives.

Having to go to the bathroom, I sneak out into the hallway to see my mother's bedroom door open a crack. I look closer to see her folding and stapling new construction paper covers on all Ape's notebooks. She never mentions it to me.

Chapter 6: My Mother's piece-of-shit Husband

I always know I have a different father from my siblings but it does not mean anything in my child life. My family is my mom, my sister, my brothers—that's my entire home world. Nearly all of the families of my friends in our low-to-no income housing project in Regina are headed by single or abandoned mothers so we are the norm.

I am playing with my Lego up in my bedroom when I hear my big sister crying loudly somewhere in our home. I slowly climb down the stairs to see her sobbing in the kitchen, holding onto Ape who is also crying. I don't know what to do or say; I don't see Mom anywhere.

"Our dad is dead," Yvette blurts out in a sob.

I am not crying but am concerned at seeing my sister so

upset. To cheer her up, I chirp, "Now Mom can get married again!" No response, more tears.

Moments later, Mom enters the back door to this emotional scene and asks what the heck is going on. Yvette manages to explain that a friend of Maurice just phoned to give the bad news of her dad being killed in a car accident. I am about to cheerily say again her marital prospects when I notice Mom's face is cool and stern. She's not crying.

She picks up the phone and makes a few expensive long-distance calls, asking about Maurice. No one from Dollard or Ponteix has heard the news.

She grabs the phone when it rings and hears the hysterical drunken laughter of Maurice: "Can't believe the kid fell for it!"

In my mother's papers are all of the letters to and from her first-born son Louis over several decades. In one, he asks her an extraordinary question that has been bugging him since his childhood:

> When and what happened that night when Maurice was lying drunk on the bed in Dollard? I remember saying to you, "Mom, I'm scared." Yvette was too terrified to say a word. Yvette and I were both hiding in the bathroom. Then we went to the Hotel next door. What happened next day? Where did Maurice go?
>
> It's lucky it did not go any further as the man was always correct in the eyes of the law and women were not much above the status of semi-slavery. The

consequences of going any further could have destroyed you with the law, as there was no battered-woman's defence then.

That is all he says and there is no answer or related comment from either our mother or Louis in any subsequent letter that I have found. There is so much I need to know about what my brother meant. Is he really hinting that Irene was thinking of killing her child-beating drunk of a husband while he lies passed out?

The following is the text of a hand-written letter by my Mom. I do not know if it is simply a first-draft of a letter sent or not sent to Maurice:

> This marriage was forced upon you the same as it was forced on me. We were never meant for each other in the first place. I only saw in you an escape from the clutches of my mother.
>
> I expected you to be a father when you knew nothing about it. Someday when you can admit your alcoholism, you will be able to understand.
>
> I want to close the door gently to our marriage vows (as they were not serious in the first place) and start a new life again. I hope and pray that my wounds and the children's wounds will be erased with time.

I ignore Mom's continuous rants against Maurice. I don't care; he's not my father. To me, he never seems like a real person. To me, he seems like a mythical figure of the worst a man can be: violent, alcoholic, dishonest, dumb as shit. To confuse my child brain, the only two photos I see of him show a muscular, handsome man.

It still amazes me to think he and Mom were only together for less than a decade yet he destroyed her entire long life, last seeing each other as he walks out the door soon after their third child is born in the late 1950s, the freakishly hairy boy only months old.

I will never know the reason she holds onto his family name forever and insists it be prominently etched on her gravestone, her maiden name in smaller letters beneath. When I take the legal steps to sever that tainted name from myself at age 22 in 1982, I am so frustrated that she will not even start a conversation about changing her name back to her beautiful and poetic maiden name.

I have the original legal document of their Decree of Judicial Separation, dated 22 May 1958 "by reason of the cruelty of the Defendant [Maurice] to the Plaintiff [Irene.]" It is noted that he did not appear at the hearing. Mom is granted sole legal custody of their three children. For child maintenance payments, he is ordered to pay her:

> One Hundred ($100.00) Dollars per month on the
> 1st day of each and every month commencing the
> 1st day of June, 1958, until further order.

Though he is ordered to pay $33.33 per child for his monthly child maintenance payments, he never pays a cent.

In the early 1980s, over two decades after Maurice walks out on his family, his three adult children do meet their father again. (Irene never again sees him after 1958 — I so regret not ever getting to see this infamous man.)

Yvette later tells me —though she is a thirty-year-old confident, happily married mother of two young girls— she is terrified of seeing her father again. She makes her brothers promise they will never leave her side for the entire time they are with Maurice. Their short visit in Calgary is as disastrous as everyone thought it would be.

That is the last time Yvette sees her father, though both sons see their father sporadically until the late-1990s with Louis writing to our mother:

> The height of hypocrisy. Maurice was trying to tell me I shouldn't take methadone. He drank all his life till a few years ago and he dares give me advice. Plus the man is an intellectual idiot.

> Maurice looks like a lonely, forlorn, old man which he is. I just pity him now. Never used his mind, and is very lonely.

> You two were a bad match right from the beginning. It could not have worked even if he didn't drink.

> I say this with no malice, but he is a bigoted, ignorant person. If I would have grown up with

25

him, I would have been ridiculing him as soon as my mind opened up around 12 or 13.

Before Maurice dies a homeless vagrant, I finally track him down to a house in Calgary where good-meaning Jehovah Witnesses are giving him shelter and support. I try to convince my two adult nieces, my sister's two daughters, to go meet their infamous grandfather.

I have never met him and am perversely interested in doing so. I say I will go along for protection. Though darkly curious, my nieces refuse, citing their mother's oft-stated pledge to her father the last time she saw him: "You will never meet my daughters."

I am disappointed. Their horrific emotional trauma of seeing this vile man in person would have made a great story.

Chapter 7: My Father and The Dancing Bubbalingas

Irene escapes Maurice and Vancouver with two kids in the early 1950s and returns to Saskatchewan. She ends up in the tiny village called Dollard in the far south-western part of Saskatchewan, only sixty miles from her childhood farm home, one million miles from her parents.

She gets the paid position of Post Mistress of the Village of Dollard at $83 every month, along with a spectacular signing bonus of free rent in a one-and-half storey house in a prime location on Railway Avenue — next to the hotel and community centre, near the school on one side and down from the five towering grain elevators. Things are looking up.

While sorting mail alone in the post office, Irene is shocked the several times she receives a letter addressed to her from Maurice, her absent but still legally-married husband. With the education and spelling of a child (in one letter he spells his daughter's name "Evet"), her illiterate husband claims he is working in the Arctic, helping to build the DEW Line — the Distant Early Warning line of radar stations that were constructed in northern Canada in the mid-1950s to warn of a Soviet missile attack.

This is true of the DEW Line. What is vague is whether or not he is actually one of the 25,000 people working on this real project. What also is true is that he never sends one promised dollar to his wife and "my boy."

The Post Office is on the full main floor of this wooden structure, the long customer counter by the front door opening directly onto the wooden sidewalk. In modern condo terms, the family living quarters are "situated in a lovely loft overlooking the spacious common area." In 1950s terms, Irene and her kids live in an open attic above a public post office.

She certainly was not expecting to hide her situation. Everyone from the village and every surrounding farm walks in her front door to get their daily mail, takes a look at that quiet red-haired boy, that little giggly girl, that very good looking young woman, then heads to coffee row to gossip.

Everyone knows every bachelor has his eyes on this good looking woman but is scared off with the weight of her children and the possibility of a surprise visit from her long-lost lunatic husband.

Even so, a bachelor farmer named Alfred strikes up a secret friendship with her — he in his late-thirties, she in her late-twenties. Despite the torrent of hate Alfred's parents would descend on him if they knew—not to mention damnation from the Roman Catholic Church—he continues this friendship with this abandoned mother of three.

In the last year of the 1950s, Alfred buys the first television set in the area, with its sole channel receiving its signal from CKCK-TV in Regina. It is set up in his tiny white wooden house with a green roof in Dollard. This is his in-town house where he spends his winters. Being a summer-only grain farmer, he has no livestock to look after year round.

The unimaginable thrill of a kid knowing someone who actually owns a television set, especially in a tiny village like Dollard, is made even more exciting for children who have special access to it.

Both Louis and Yvette have childhood memories of the many times they would be brought over to Alfred's house: sitting on the living room rug, mesmerized for hours at the one-station television. Louis and Yvette are told to look after their little hairy brother and to never ever disturb Mom and Alfred having tea in the other room.

In a letter from Louis to our mother, he writes,

> I can remember going to his place and we would watch TV and the late movie. Yvette and I would sleep in the basement which lifted with a trap door.

Deducting exactly nine months from my birth date gives me 06 November 1959. I look up the date in the TV Guide archives to see what shows are being broadcast on that Friday evening.

One is the premiere of an episode of The Twilight Zone titled 'Escape Clause,' and it is quite likely I am conceived while Rod Serling is talking to my sister and brothers out in the living room:

"Submitted for your approval ..." a lonely mother with no way out.

My mother must really be in love because, after the horrible disaster of her husband, I would think she would be quite jaded towards men.

Further evidence she is blindly in love is her full belief in Alfred's 'Big Promise.' He tells her he is unlikely to be able to have children, but if by miracle she does become pregnant, he will marry her and they will all become one big happy family.

A miracle happens and she is pregnant and when Alfred announces this to his recently-widowed mother, she gives her son an ultimatum: marry this woman with your bastard child and relinquish all claim to the family farm forever, or get rid of her and inherit everything.

At age 38, Alfred, in love for the first time in his life, sides with his mother.

The following is transcribed from a carbon copy of a hand-written letter from my mother to my father. I know nothing of this letter until I read it in her papers after her death. I know she left this copy for me.

It was in November 1959 that you made your big promise to me, and I was so desperate and stupid enough to fall for it and be taken advantage of. Your promise was that if you could father a child (seeing you had some doubts due to an incident of the past), we would get married as soon as I would become pregnant.

I thought you were different than Maurice, that you had some love and devotion in you.

After the months went by, I realized that you had no intention of ever marrying me. I thought about an abortion many times, but somehow couldn't go through with it.

I believe that it's through my strong belief in the Christian faith, that there is a better life to come, which has enabled me to persevere. And not to give in to the thoughts of suicide during my times of deep depression.

The village does not have a hospital so I am born ten miles east in Shaunavon Union Hospital. I have no idea who is taking care of my siblings when I enter the world. Chances are, responsible ten-year-old Louis and nine-year-old Yvette are at home alone taking care of four-year-old Ape, with neighbours checking in.

When my mother returns home, possibly driving herself with me on the passenger floor, I am quickly baptised in Dollard's Sainte-Jeanne d'Arc Catholic Church with the missing Maurice listed as my father.

Everyone knows I am the "bastard child" of Irene and Alfred —a real, legal term at the time meaning born out of wedlock— but everyone, including the priest, pretends otherwise.

I am baptised into the Catholic Church as Alfred David G.

Alfred, the name of my real father with no one saying that out loud; David, the name of my mother's grandfather, a name she has always liked; G, the family name of the violent lunatic my mother is still legally married to.

I never knew why, but she will carry that poisonous surname from her wedding day to her death over sixty years later. I too carry that name, albeit for only my first twenty-two. In 1982, without warning my mom, I legally change my names from Alfred David G to David Robert Loblaw. Though confused at my choice of names, she is pleased with my decision.

Four decades later, Mom applies to the Government of Saskatchewan Department of Vital Statistics to have my official 1960 Record of Live Birth altered to show Alfred as my real father, not Maurice.

It is only when I am 46 do I finally become a legal bastard.

I do not know if this is a quirky French-Canadian way of naming children or a quirky Western Canada French-Canadian way of naming children, but everyone in my family has their middle name first on our government-issued birth certificates.

Mine has Alfred first, but I am called David every day of my life. Mom's birth certificate has Rose first, but she is Irene. My oldest brother has Maurice, he is Louis. Yvette has Rita-Marie, she is always Yvette. Ape ate his so I don't know how his names are listed on his birth certificate.

With the impossibility of life in a small village for an abandoned woman with four children, Irene knows she must leave. Exactly a month after my birth, her sister Eva and her husband, Uncle George, drive from Regina to Dollard to help pack up as many of our belongings as will fit in their car and trailer.

In actual fact, everything cannot fit, so my father is asked to load items in one of his pickup trucks and follow everyone to the big city of Regina. After unloading the possessions of his lover and new-born child, he gets back in his truck and drives alone back to the farm and his mother.

In my mother's wallet is a promissory note from Alfred for five hundred dollars. Several months later, he does indeed pay this flat-rate to my mother for his total financial share in raising me. He will never again pay any type of child support directly to her — just this one-time payoff for my entire upbringing, which works out to $2.31 per month for eighteen years.

(It ticks me off when I do the math and realize The Court in 1958 ordered Maurice to pay Irene a hundred dollars a month to raise their three children of Louis, Yvette, and Ape; while in 1960, orders my father to pay a little over two dollars a month for me.)

My father and mother never live together, not even for a day. From my birth until their deaths over forty years later, they live apart, in their own little houses, a three-hour car trip away from each other.

Their self-hate relationship would have made a much more heart-warming and powerful story if their love affair had been severed by war or class or ethnic differences: the drama of big stories. But both are born on family farms in southwest Saskatchewan, born of French Canadian blood, raised in large farm families, fluent in French and English, only a few years in age difference, both immersed in The One True Church.

Though there is nothing keeping them apart, they both spend their lives alone, far beyond the lifespan of their disapproving parents, neither ever having any other type of relationship for the rest of their lives.

I find a two-sentence letter from my father to my mother from 1983. He's 61, she's 52:

> Glad to see your name in last Thursday's Leader Post as a winner in the O.K. Economy Store contest. Hope this happens occasionally, as it is the only way I have of knowing that you are still

alive, still in Regina and still go under your same name.

Another tiny letter, four years later, at age 65, he writes:
Drove by your place a number of times, its a lot better than mine although I am well pleased with what I have now.

The only time my wife meets Alfred is in 1993 when we visit him in his tiny house in Dollard, the place where I was most likely conceived. He is a congenial host, giving us an extensive tour of his tidy home. As he leads us out of his bedroom/office, we pause to focus on a weathered, curled-up black and white photograph stuck in the corner of his mirror. It's Irene, in the late-1950s, soon after he met her.

From a letter from Louis to our mother, describing his child memory from 1962:
Even in Arcola Ave [our first house in Regina], Alfred came over several times. I can still remember being awake one night when you and him were on the chesterfield in the living room. You were crying desperately. I don't recall seeing him coming back after that. Was that when you ended it?

Randomly throughout my childhood in the 1960s, Alfred does send me extravagant birthday or Christmas gifts. One is the biggest three-panel chemistry set ever made, filled with beakers, test-tubes, blow torch, and lots of fun and exciting chemicals in blue plastic bottles: sodium ferrocyanide, tannic acid, potassium chloride.

As a child, I know nothing about my father except his name is Alfred. I never think about him; I don't even know what a Dad is, nor do I care.

One day, without prompting, my sister tells me the whole story. She explains that his name is indeed Alfred, and that he is in vaudeville. His act is called 'Freddie and the Dancing BubbaLingas' which features him as a comedian holding a giant sharp pin in front of a group of gorgeous cancan dancers wearing nothing but balloons. They travel around North America in a comedy show with Alfred telling jokes, chasing the women, popping a balloon whenever he gets a laugh. The more laughter from the audience, the more nudity from the Dancing BubbaLingas. I would love to have been able to see that show.

In a letter I find in my mother's papers after her death, my brother Louis says,

> David had written me a letter asking me questions that Yvette had told him if they were true. I hadn't realized how much she exaggerated. I told him Yvette looked at the world like a soap opera. She was a romantic and lived in a dream world.

I am eight years old the first time I remember seeing my

35

father. Afterwards, I see my mother the most angry I will see her, ever.

In 1968, in a huge honour, Mom has been chosen to be a tenant representative of our housing project to fly to a conference in Ottawa — all expenses paid by the federal government. A single mom of four being asked her opinions of low-income public housing is one of the biggest events in her life.

Yvette teases her that maybe Prime Minister Pierre Trudeau, a bachelor at the time, has arranged for her to fly out to see him. I cry when she says that Mom might marry Pierre; I cry not because of the man—I really like his long hair—but that we would have to move far away to Ottawa and I am frantic not knowing if I can take all of my moon rocket models with me.

Mom entrusts seventeen-year-old Yvette with my care during her short absence, foolishly forgetting to tell her daughter she cannot take her little brother on a two-hour bus ride to my birthplace so she can party with her cousin Carol.

Upon arrival in Shaunavon, Yvette phones Alfred out-of-the-blue to ask if he would like to take care of his eight year old son for a day or two. I cannot imagine what Alfred thinks of this stunning phone call. He has not seen me since I was a toddler, ever since my mother finally severed contact with him after two years of continual failed promises of him saying he was going to reverse his decision and marry her, even if it meant giving up the farm.

I have a great time with this man called Alfred, a man my

sister says is my dad — whatever that means. He has an interesting little house with a trap door in the middle of his kitchen floor, which goes down to a cool root cellar. He has a metal filing cabinet with a real safe built into it; he even tells me the combination so I can open the vault—nothing but boring papers inside. He buys me an Etch-a-Sketch, teasing me to draw the Olympic rings. He buys me big greasy delicious hamburgers and ice-cold Cokes from the bar in the hotel; sure is dark and smoky and strange in there, even in the daytime, and I don't know why those men at the bar were staring when Alfred brought me in.

I eat chips and liquorice, sitting on the living room rug watching TV. I spend hours in front of his bookcase filled with decades of National Geographic magazines, all monthly sequential, flipping through every one for anything about the space program. As a self-appointed consultant to the Apollo program, I need to keep informed.

In Alfred's green pickup truck, we drive out on dusty roads to visit many parts of his farm, stopping to take photos of me standing in his endless golden wheat fields. Alfred has lots of trucks and fascinating farm equipment. Sitting behind me, he lets me wobbly drive his bright green John Deere tractor a little ways down a path.

He shows me the Dollard Cemetery where he cuts the grass and does general upkeep; he does not show me the graves of any of my ancestors on his side. He gives me a tour of Sainte-Jeanne d'Arc Catholic Church, failing to mention he did not attend my baptism there eight years ago.

Only after Yvette's and my fun bus ride home the next day and I am up in my bedroom, blocking out Mom yelling furiously at my sister downstairs, do I wonder why I did not get to meet the Dancing BubbaLingas.

PART TWO: SCHOOL

Chapter 8: Everyone Goes to School

Though 1966 is a milestone year for me as I enter school for the first time in Grade One (there was no kindergarten), it is a much more momentous year for my mother. She is one of the first students to attend Miller Composite High, the newly-built Catholic high school.

With only a Grade Ten education going back to 1947, she is making the scary and courageous step to re-enter high school at age 35. She describes this twenty-year gap as feeling like Rip Van Winkle, having slept for two decades to awake to a new and confusing world. Made even more bizarre for Mom is the fact she will be attending the same high school as her teenage daughter — Yvette will be in Grade Ten, she in Grade Eleven.

(The year prior, my sister did her Grade Nine in the basement of Little Flower Church, in what was called Bosco High School and was dissolved when Miller High opened.)

The following is written about us in the Fall 1966 Catholic School System newsletter, Spotlight on Regina's Separate Schools:

> September was back-to-school time for the entire G[x] family. The two youngest boys entered Grades 1 and 4 at St. Thomas School. An older son entered Grade 11 at Campion College. Yvette, 14, and Mrs. Irene G[x], mother of all four, were among Miller Composite School's first students.

Mom and Yvette also hit newspapers nation-wide with the

41

headline "Mother Daughter Scholars" on 20 October 1966:

REGINA (CP) —Yvette G[x], 14, had company when she entered Grade 10 at Miller Composite High School this fall. Her mother, Mrs. Irene G[x], 35, entered Grade 11.

Members of the school board approved Mrs. G[x]'s application. She had not attended school since she received her Grade 10 certificate 19 years ago at Ponteix, Sask.

A mother of four, including a son at college, Mrs. G[x] hopes to go on to university and eventually teach home economics.

"After all, I've had enough experience," she said.

I find it impossible to imagine what it felt like for my mother to go back to high school at age thirty-five, yet still have all of the household burdens and worries of a single mother of four on welfare. To me, as a six-year-old, it is perfectly normal each morning to see my mother and sister get dressed in their high school uniform—grey skirt, white top, grey vest—and wait at the bus stop.

I have no idea the terror my mother is going though trying to adjust to school life amongst teenagers, one being her increasingly rebellious daughter who wants nothing to do with her embarrassing mother who walks the same school hallways as her.

As an adult, one of Yvette's biggest regrets is how she treated our mother when they were in high school together. In a letter dated in the mid-1980s, she writes:

> You seemed so old to us when you returned to school. No other Mom embarrassed their kids by attending the same highschool as them! We were so proud but made it so miserably difficult for you. Kids can be such rotters!
>
> On reflection, I regret my obstinate "coming of age" and how deeply I must of hurt you. I apologize, belatedly.

Though Louis is in the same grade as our mother, he does not attend nearby Miller High School with her and his sister. Instead, based on his advanced academic standing and multiple scholarships, he is enrolled at Campion, the elite private Catholic boys school in the richie-rich south end of town.

He refuses to help our mother with any type of homework, which is an infuriating source of frustration for her. With so many family and financial pressures in her life, she struggles with the torrent of many new school subjects and desperately needs help. He freezes her out.

Much later, Louis writes this in a letter to her:

> Remember in Grade 11, I think you were close to a nervous breakdown, if not in fact having one.
>
> You would virtually refuse to talk to me and when I would wake up in the morning there would be articles on the table from magazines telling what psychopaths were. I have lost track on how many there were there that you left for me to read. I

would read them and then destroy them; at 16 years old without any knowledge of psychology, those articles were devastating to me. They were obviously meant for me.

I just did not understand then though what the hell was going on, and because you ignored me, I did the same to you.

Things straightening out in Grade 12 once we adjusted to our way of life and I'm guessing school work became easier for you.

I am eight when I watch Mom receive her high school diploma on the stage at Miller High School, quite a surreal experience. Dressed in a flowing white graduation gown and starched cap, she is beaming with pride (most likely purged at her next Confession as pride is a sin.)

With her diploma in hand, she starts a decade of night and summer university classes, culminating in her Bachelor of Education degree from the University of Regina.

For my mother's funeral, I create a booklet in which I write:

With the family receiving the many condolences upon Irene's death, most people state how tough a life she had, how much hardship and sorrow she endured. Yes, this is all true. But what we must emphasize is how strong and determined she was, how she overcame nearly every social, religious, educational, and monetary obstacle to become one of the most successful 'Single Moms' any of us will ever know.

Going from an uneducated single mother of four on welfare to earning a university degree, becoming a teacher, and buying her own house is a magnificent triumph that she did all herself. We were along for the ride but she did all the work.

Chapter 9: Sister Margaret

Shortly before my mother's death, she tells me that one of her biggest regrets was not being able to take me to my First Day of School. I don't feel bad about it, because I know for her it was also a big day: her first day of school, entering Grade 11 after a twenty-year absence.

I sense the dread my mother must have felt when she realizes the only available person to take me is Ape.

I don't remember entering St. Thomas School for the first time. Ape was probably running, with me trying to keep up. All I recall is suddenly being in the middle of a noisy, swirling crowd of kids in the main hallway—me, the only one motionless, not knowing what to do or where to go. Ape has indeed brought me to school, but has just abandoned me.

The chaos and noise empties out to me standing alone in the gigantic empty silent hall, not knowing what the hell to do.

I jump out of my skin when suddenly a deep growly man's

45

voice demands, "Name?" I turn around to see a scary figure which still haunts me to this day. In a classroom doorway is a towering figure in a black hooded robe, its face ringed in white, a huge crucifix where a belt-buckle should be.

"Boy. Come here." I have seen nuns before but none had ever talked to me. They are scarier the closer you get to them.

"Name?" I cannot talk. She looks at her list, looks up, "David?" I nod. She points into her classroom.

The entire school is filled with children everywhere. Every classroom is crammed in straight rows with a wide variety of desks gathered from all over the Separate School Division: from shiny new metal ones with no inkwell hole to the heavily-scratched, classic wooden ones with a pull-out drawer for your books under the seat.

The aisles between the rows are so narrow, the sleeves of Sister Margaret's habit hit us in the face as she swishes by to hit a talker in the back of the room.

It is quite unnerving when I am sweating an arithmetic test and suddenly sense a dark presence beside me. I slowly turn my head to be face-to-face with tortured, dead Jesus Christ: the huge crucifix at Sister's waist. I look closely at his face, praying he will tell me the number I am looking for. He never does. He doesn't even look up.

Above my Grade One classroom's blackboard are large, printed pale-green alphabet cards in the proper upper case and lower case. Any deviation from these at any time results in an ear pull or a slap on the head.

Beside the blackboard, in descending order, is a photo of the Vicar of Christ, Pope Paul VI; a photo of our Sovereign, forty-year-old Queen Elizabeth II; and the old Red Ensign flag. Our school was reluctant to say goodbye to the Red Ensign and kept it around until being forced to change it to our new red maple leaf flag for Canada's Centennial Year in 1967.

Being a small kid, my assigned desk is at the front. Though I am terrified of Sister Margaret sitting at her desk a few feet in front of me, she is much more interested and involved in the souls going to Hell in the back of the classroom.

In another life and era and gender, she may have been the greatest pitcher in baseball history. Her accuracy when she bolts up and throws her oversize white chalk is astounding. Seeing it painfully bounce off the forehead of a yapper at the back is an eerie thrill for me. One kid reacts like a whiny baby when she does a direct hit into one of his eyes.

Throughout every day, when someone does something wrong or against the rules or is just stupid, Sister gives the offender an instant slap on the side of the head or a quick pull on an ear. Even as a perfect boy who does not talk, I get a few of these. The worst offenders per day do not get an immediate penalty. Their names are printed in chalk in the corner of the blackboard and must simmer in terror until the end of the school day to discover their punishment.

My morbid fascination rises every time someone is singled out, a guaranteed front-row seat to every execution. Though the pronouncement is always Sister's penalty-by-ruler, the number of times she will strap your outstretched hand is not pre-announced. It will be directly proportional to the severity of your sin against God. (I have yet to see the Ruler Punishment Chart but I am sure it is somewhere in the library.)

What fascinates and somewhat creeps me out — now, not then—is how I eagerly await the end of each day to watch the public flagellation of my classmates: the pasty faces of those waiting in line, the slap-snap sound of the ruler on their hands, again and again, the wincing of child faces in adult pain, the howls and the tears, the banishment of evil from our world.

The first day of every school year starts with roll call, each of us in alphabetical turn responding with a raised arm and a happy "here!" But it always comes to an abrupt stop when the teacher gets to the latter half of the Gs and sees my last name.

This is where, each year, my new teacher takes a breath, and prepares herself for Ape's little brother: the hellion of her classroom for the next year.

"David G ...?" the teacher bravely calls out.

I put up my hand.

"Is David G here?" she says, slowly standing up to look to the big boys at the back of the classroom.

Immediately in front of her teacher desk, below her field of view, is a skinny little kid frantically waving his arm.

"For the last time," she announces, most likely with fingers crossed, "Is David G here?"

I am still waving, holding one arm up at the elbow with my

other when she finally looks down to notice the little thin kid, middle row, front seat.

"I'm David G," I say.

Each teacher has a different yelp:

"Oh, my Lord!"

"Praise be to Heaven!"

Or a silent raising of her crucifix for a kiss of gratitude before collapsing back down on her chair.

Chapter 10: St. Thomas

My elementary school opens in September 1955 and is built to last forever. St. Thomas is a classic two-floor brick and stone building: solid, rectangular, functional. I first enter it in 1966.

The beautiful main doors, all metal and glass, are only for teachers, parents, adults, and the janitor. If a kid ever had the guts to walk up the steps and enter those doors, he or she would see a beautiful stone dual staircase with a dozen steps on the right up to the upper floor, a dozen steps on the left down to the lower floor.

The upper floor has five classrooms, along with a narrow Nurse's Station and The Principal's Office with its direct door into the Grade Eight classroom. The lower floor has three classrooms, and the boys' and girls' washrooms.

It also has a door to The Janitor's Room, which leads to a

mythical world of hot steam and loud clanking noises. It is also where a kid is sent when even the nuns have had enough. Ape says he has his own special stool in The Janitor's Room.

Us kids enter St. Thomas via the playground side, in through either the boys' door or the girls' door. Everyone is dared at one time or another to run in the other gender's door but no one to my knowledge has ever done so. Everyone knows that is how homosexuals are created.

After opening the boys' door (the only one I know), we run twenty feet down a concrete hallway then do a sharp, right-hand 180-turn down another twenty-foot hallway. This is meant as a crowd-slowing devise but rarely works. If someone trips in the mayhem—usually Mute or Hamster—they get trampled by the avalanche of oncoming boots.

This hallway mini-maze opens wide into the boys' washroom: a long row of urinals on the far side, a long row of sinks on the close. In the corner is one stall with a toilet. One must never, ever use it. We are taught to always do our duties in the privacy of our home bathroom, not to poop in public like a Protestant.

The entire boys' washroom is fully accessible and patrolled by the Sisters who have no hesitation to bang on the stall door of a child so unfortunate they had to go number two at school.

"Who's in there? What are you doing? Hurry up!"

If the vile excreter happens to make a bodily sound in the stall, heaven help him.

"Stop that now! Jesus frowns on bathroom sounds!"

The playground of St. Thomas School is enormous, and out there on the patchy grass field, we are free of the nuns. We are on our own. They never police it, only reluctantly going out when someone's arm is snapped or some fool is bleeding too much or the new kid won't wake up.

Ringing the entire field and school is chain-link fencing with openings at each corner. These are not gates, just four-foot gaps in the fence. The opening on the northeast corner, the one touching busy Park Street, finally gets a zigzag of fencing to stop kids from running straight off the playground into traffic. This child-slowing fencing is quite effective in reducing the number of monthly child/car collisions and lessens the frequency our Elmer the Safety Elephant flag is lowered.

On the other side of the playground's south fence is a ditch, a railway track, and a highway. The railway is the Canadian Pacific line from Regina southeast to Stoughton. Everyone brags that this 132 kilometre section is the longest stretch of dead-straight track in the world. (It's not.) The highway is the 33, parallel to the rail line all the way.

And on the other side of the highway are the Protestants. Lots of them. A horde of screaming sinners in a school called Arcola, not named after a Saint like ours but simply the city street the school sits beside. Protestants have no pizzazz.

Sister Margaret repeatedly and constantly warns us in many ways: "Never EVER play with a Protestant. Never talk to one, don't even get close to them." This is constantly drilled into us all day, every day. A mantra that soon loses all meaning.

51

Until one Saturday matinee at the Met Theatre when it pops into my head. I am bouncing in my seat amongst hundreds of wild kids waiting for Fantastic Voyage to start — everyone yelling, screaming, popcorn boxes being flattened to wing at Johnny Sandison's head as he makes a pre-movie draw on stage.

Muffling the hysteria is Sister's clear, deep voice: "Never talk to a Protestant, don't even get close to them. David, you'll go to Hell!"

Frightened, I suddenly see devils all around me in this enormous movie theatre. I look around at the mayhem and get cold with fear: I cannot tell who the Protestants are. I have talked and joked with many and I cannot tell which ones are which now. This is terrible.

Johnny makes a quick exit, the lights dim, the cartoons start. I crouch low in my chair to decide what to do next. A quick dash out the side exit makes sense. But what if the Protestants follow me to the back alley to beat me up?

I don't know what to do until I hear a faint voice behind me: "My brother says you get to see Rachel Welch's boobs."

This completely displaces everything in my head.

I bolt up straight, wide-eyed, knocking over my popcorn. In a trance, I mouth, "Oh my, oh my, gonna get to see them, finally gonna get to see them ..."

Chapter 11: Hippo Hunt

David is a very popular name for newborns in the 1950s and early 60s. In every gathering I am in—school, church, summer camp, science fair—there are always multiple Davids and I must add my last initial when saying or writing my name.

Especially when I enter Grade Three, a split Grade 3 and 4 classroom with a trio of Davids, me being one of the two in the lower grade. All my assignments, notebooks, textbooks, and science projects must contain 'David G, Grade 3' as I never want to be confused with 'David G, Grade 4,' the silent giant in the largest desk at the back of the classroom, the one we can tell what he had for lunch by looking at the front of his shirt.

His outside name is Hippo, a nickname born one recess on the school playground when we are all standing around bored. As I recall, I am leaning on the green wooden bike rack, listening to some older boys discuss that if a man cannot get his wife pregnant, the doctor will do it to her instead. With my head spinning with this information, everyone in the playground hears someone yell "Hippo Hunt!"

In some freaky mind-control event, we all simultaneously turn to look directly at David G, Grade 4. Sensing something bad is about to happen, he starts to quickly waddle away towards the far end of the playground, his fat legs barely able to keep his forward momentum going.

Chasing and piling up on him, in some sort of insane Lord of the Flies moment, his chubby knees buckle from the weight of us kids on top of him and he falls to the ground, everyone

53

scrambling not to be crushed underneath. A ring of kids standing around the fallen hippo, everyone kicking and kicking and kicking him until someone yells, "Sister's coming!" We scatter like cockroaches to a switched-on light.

My only other close encounter with Hippo is when he hands out invitations to his birthday party. I always go to every birthday party I am invited to. Yvette taught me to never turn down free food or booze.

Mrs. Hippo greets me at their front door and shows me the huge dining room table she has decorated for her son's birthday: balloons, party hats, Batman paper plates, a gigantic white cake, big jug of Kool-Aid.

I take a seat and say hi to Hippo sitting at the head of the table, putting on my matching cardboard party hat. It is Hippo and me and a dozen empty chairs.

Between sips of Kool-Aid, we talk about Batman and how cool it was to see the real Batmobile when it was displayed at the OK Economy Loblaw grocery store the previous summer.

His mom keeps looking out the front window and checking her watch.

We agree the guys pretending to be the real Batman and Robin with the Batmobile were so lame. "A couple of fems," we laugh.

Mrs. Hippo comes back to the table and cuts two big pieces of cake. As she puts each one on its plate, I see she has done what I have always asked my mother to do but she never has the creativity to do: coins are sprinkled throughout the cake —

all quarters too, no cheapo dimes and nickels.

After wolfing down this delicious cake, being sure to suck my quarters clean, I say see-ya to Hippo and walk directly to Jim's Lucky Dollar Store with my seventy-five cent bonanza.

Later, when Mom asks me if I thanked David's mom for the cake and Kool-Aid, I say she was lying down in the dark on the living room couch when I left and did not want to wake her up. She was sniffling and sounded like she had a bad cold.

Chapter 12: Mouth the Words

Aside from weekly Mass in the gym, we have little contact with the parish Priest. He does not teach any classes and we never see him outside of church except for special events, the big one being The Christmas Concert. This is when he invades St. Thomas and usurps the nuns with his superior musical talent. He only wants heavenly voices in the choirs and he is the sole judge.

One by one, we are asked to rehearse a song and sing it in front of him and the class.

"Row, row, row your boat … gently … um, down stream … Merry, merry, merry … ummm …"

The Priest races towards me at the blackboard, sticks his face right into mine, "You! — " tapping a finger on my forehead, "Mouth the words."

In the many years Mom watches me sing in the Christmas choir, I never had the courage to tell her I was the angel just silently opening and closing its mouth.

Standing in front of the class and forgetting the eighteen words to the simplest song in the English language is ample proof music is not my best subject in school. I just do not understand music; it is a foreign language forever hidden from me. I also find it unsettling as it is the only activity that the nuns seem to really enjoy and the only time corporal punishment is fully suspended.

We have two music classes per week. I do well in the classroom instruction hour where we learn about whole notes, half notes, and all music notation. I am fascinated watching Sister draw the musical staff on the blackboard with her five-chalk rastrum. I practice drawing a perfect treble clef in my music notebook, but am disappointed I am never asked to come up to the board to draw one.

The practical music hour is when we march down to the Science Room (ridiculously called the Science & Music Room) to get our musical ability judged. Based on these arbitrary and heavily-biased assessments, we are positioned for the rest of the year in a designated spot. I am assigned to a low bench away from everyone else, in the corner with two musical losers.

It is made emotionally complicated when my classmate Louise, a piano prodigy and overdeveloped in many ways for her age, is the one assigned to hand out the many instruments to everyone. There is not much left when beautiful Louise

56

finally gets to us in the corner. She is holding up two triangles, their glint in her deep green eyes. She hands one to Loser #1 and the other to Loser #2, then walks away.

From across the room I hear Sister say, "Oh, I dunno, give him the blocks."

Louise returns and straps wooden blocks onto my palms, her soft red hair caressing my forearms — dreaming of playing a duet together soon.

Chapter 13: S is for Science

I love everything about the Science Fair at our school, and spend many months preparing for the big event. It is my moment to shine, my showcase, my public stage to show everyone the work I have done for NASA in the previous year.

Each year, I highlight another fascinating aspect of the Apollo moon missions. Each year, my face lights up when my teacher sits me down to ask if I have thought about possibly doing something different this year.

"Absolutely!" I say. "I'm going to build a model of the lunar rover (moon buggy) to show how the astronauts of Apollo 17 fixed the broken fender with duct tape and a map!" Every teacher sighs at my depth of knowledge.

In the school gymnasium on Science Fair Day, I love standing in front of my tri-panel cardboard display of brilliance.

I must tolerate the afternoon portion where my audience is my fellow classmates: the dullards who do not understand the basics of lunar orbit insertion, but would rather know where astronauts go to the bathroom.

I distract them by showing a tiny flipbook I've hand-drawn of the many stages of a moon mission, from launch to splashdown. I smile as the girls slowly back away in dreamy wonderment.

The evening of the Science Fair is where I shine: adults with really challenging questions and unending praise, though it does tick me off when I am about to demonstrate the Command Module/Service Module separation and my audience runs off to watch the stupid show-offs start their volcanos.

The person who ruins the Science Fair every year is Brian the Brain, in yet another ridiculous circus act. I do not even go over to his project in the corner of the gym, the one with the crowd, lest he think I am there to poke holes in his thesis. I do not know many details, but one year I hear he creates a solar-powered non-polluting water filtration system that can make any water drinkable. It is supposed to "help" people in Africa; obviously not as much as the space program. His dad probably built it for him.

Every year Brian the Brain and a dozen others are chosen from St. Thomas School to participate in the city-wide Science Fair. It will take place at the classic Armouries Building, a beautiful brick fortress on Elphinstone Street. Though it is my life ambition to display at the huge Regina Science Fair, I do not feel bad I have never been chosen. I realize the school officials cannot nominate me knowing I am under contract with NASA and my sweeping all the science awards would seriously demoralize the lesser students.

When I confide to my sister my desire to display at the city Science Fair, she naturally comes up with a solution. She says a project unrelated to the moon missions will legally and technically allow me to participate. Knowing I have looked through her biology books, she asks if there is anything in there that sparks my interest for a science project.

"Absolutely!" I say. "Flatworms!"

Flatworms are exactly what their name implies: worms that are flat. Us biological scientists call them planarians, a member of the genus Planaria within the family Planariidae. For my experiments, I will be using the brownish species, Girardia tigrina.

What makes these flatworms so fascinating to me and everyone within hearing distance is their incredible regenerative capability: slice a planarian's body in half at the waist and each half will grow the missing half —the top creating a new bottom, the bottom creating a new top— thereby making two full flatworms.

The moment I tell Mom of my ingenious project, she starts making phone calls to high school and university biology teachers to find out how we can get some planarians for my project. As she drives around town getting my science materials, she must cry tears of joy at the thought of her youngest son winning the Regina Science Fair then onwards to a Nobel Prize.

After many months of preparation, of obtaining the planarians and petri dishes, of a few trial runs, I am ready for the St. Thomas Science Fair.

My experiments are perfect, with full documentation of my slicing of these flatworms in many different ways and real-life examples of the regenerative result. The long line-up at my microscope in the gymnasium on Science Fair Day to view my specimens far exceeds what the pathetic Brian the Brain could ever hope for.

With my unmistakable brilliance I am of course chosen to participate in next month's city-wide Science Fair.

My St. Thomas planarians will not live much longer, so I am ready to start slicing again with a new batch, this time in even more varied permutations.

It is now a week away from the big Regina Science Fair and all my new specimens are starting to regenerate their missing parts exactly as expected: sliced head to tail, each side recreating its mirror image; sliced in three, each recreating two-thirds of itself. Everyone finds my experiments fascinating. My family is mesmerized at my non-stop talking about this project, my best one ever.

Six times a day, I document my experiment's progress. Not all the planarians regenerate their parts: many shrivel up and die, others survive the amputation and are happy to live with half a body. As I look through my microscope, mere days away, I am astounded I have achieved the near-impossible: one of the flatworms whose head I have sliced in half—from top of its head to its neck—has re-grown the other half of each head, while still attached to a single body.

It's a living Y! I have created a Siamese twin flatworm. There is no doubt in anyone's mind that this is the year Brian the Brain gets crushed.

The crowds are enormous in the Armouries during the Science Fair afternoons and evenings. This is before the era of VCRs, so I am not able to record the 6 o'clock CKCK-TV News whose top story would be my project.

The tough thing about being a solo presenter at a science fair is I do not have any opportunity to walk around the hall to take a look at my competition. I heard Brian the Brain had to get special permission to bring "his" project in through the loading docks. That is a lot of trouble for a big pile of junk, whatever it is — something about a scale model of a mountainous river valley with hidden water tanks showing the visible effects of erosion over a millennium. All show, no science — unlike a two-headed flatworm.

After talking to the thousands of people who walk by my project and are drawn into the wonderful world of planaria, I try to not let their mountain of compliments cloud my sole purpose of being here: the advancement of science, not the winning of a prize. Though, I must admit, trying to shut out thinking about the prizes is quite difficult.

First prize is the full twenty-two volume set of the World Book Encyclopaedia AND the full-colour three-volume World Book Atlas AND the World Book Dictionary.

Second prize is the Atlas and Dictionary.

Third prize is just the Dictionary.

At the end of the Science Fair, it is award time and though I brace myself, I am slightly shocked and annoyed when Brian the Brain gets First Prize. (Yvette later says it's all politics; I have no idea what she means.) No matter — I am looking forward to flipping through my full-colour three-volume Atlas in a few minutes.

I am anxiously sitting on my metal chair in the audience, on an aisle seat so I can quickly get to the podium. I learn this from watching the Academy Awards and the crazy long time some winners take to get up there.

Things turn dark and awful when I do not hear my name announced for Second Place. I see a girl take my place at the podium. This is terrible; how can this be? Second place, with the Atlas and Dictionary, stolen from me and I now have to settle for third.

Taking deep, slow breaths like Mom taught me, I calm myself. Coming in third is not the end of the world, but it is a tad embarrassing.

I wobbly stand up when my name is announced and someone hits me on the back of my head, yelling at me to sit down. I turn around to look at this lunatic, who is busy adjusting his camera. Everyone is clapping and when I turn back to the stage, some weird kid is being handed the Dictionary and my Third Prize.

The whole hall goes dark. Sounds are muffled like being underwater in the tub. I hit the chair in a flop of disbelief and disappointment, my head dropping between my knees. There's no way I lost everything. It's impossible.

"Go up, go up there, your name's called."

Someone is poking my shoulder. I lift my head and when I try to focus, my teachers are looking at me, and pointing to the stage where a man is waiting.

"Get up there, David! You got fourth," someone says.

I am so confused as I stumble up to the podium. There is no such thing as Fourth Prize. I get more curious the closer I get. The man truly looks like he is holding a book with World Book colours. I am so confused: the Encyclopaedia set has been given away, the Atlas has been given away, the Dictionary has been given away. There is nothing else.

Everything is a blur to me: getting my limp hand shaken, being given a book, getting a shove off the stage. It is only when I am seated do I have a chance to take a closer look at my prize. I am in silent awe at the World Book cover and when I see what is written on its spine, I am bewildered.

It's an S. I won the S from the 1972 set of World Book Encyclopaedia. Just the S. For science I suppose.

When I show my prize to my sister, she laughs and laughs and laughs. She says that is the weirdest thing she has ever seen. I don't think it's all that bad.

Over the next few years, none of my other science projects or other school assignments bring me as close to fame as the one at this Science Fair. Though I continue to create many memorable projects in all my school assignments on a wide variety of subjects —saccharin, salamanders, Saturn, Scotland, smallpox, Joseph Stalin, sulfur— my heart remains with those two-headed flatworms, my friends, those amazing planarians. I shed a tear when I wash them down the drain.

Chapter 14: My Sports Legacy

"Line up! We're picking teams!" is the last thing I want to hear out on the St. Thomas playground at recess, especially when I've found several dead beetles and am fashioning little crosses out of toothpicks to use in their upcoming burial ceremony by the schoolyard fence.

It is always the same two boys — the toughest guys, the ones who are each other's sworn enemy — who are the team captains and who do all the picking. I put up my hand to object to this flagrant lack of democracy and to suggest team captains should be rotated based on last name or perhaps a random lottery based on assigned numbers. When no one cedes the floor to me, I decide it would be better to write up a report on electoral reform and present it to the group at a later time.

(I also note we should invest in uniforms instead of the primitive 'shirts and skins.')

Surprisingly, I am never picked first, or second, or third, or fourth, or fifth. Far down the line, when I am finally chosen, it's not by my proper name but "And-the-rest-of-them."

I love soccer the best as no one has assigned roles — dozens of crazed kids running around kicking a ball — and I can get back to my funeral services by the fence.

I hate the question "Are you a team player?" as it forces me to lie by nodding my head. But I'm not. I prefer solo sports such as cycling, boxing, wrestling, dodgeball, and the one where I shine: track and field — high-jump, 100 yard dash, the 440, and especially the super-cool sounding Hop, Skip, & Jump (the zip of its name later dulled to the triple jump.)

Though a distant second to Science Fair Day in April, Track & Field Day every June is an exciting time of the year for me. This is where I strut my stuff, wind in my hair, grabbing the eye of every girl.

And there would not be a Track & Field Day without my prowess. The teachers choose me and two other highly-skilled boys for the most prestigious honour: preparing the enormous playground for all of the athletic events to be held.

Us three are let out of classes the afternoon before and from the classroom windows, everyone jealously watches us sensually saunter out to the grass, each pushing our chalk marking machine. Up and down the playground we go, creating a masterful white tapestry of straight or curved lanes and high-jump perimeters — all based on the to-scale graph paper diagram I gave to my teacher, who, instantly realizing its worth, places it in her bottom drawer for archival purposes.

Taking a break at recess to get a drink of water at the fountain, we see giggly girls admiring us, whispering, "hey chalk boys!" We wipe our powdery-white faces and wink back at them before returning to work on the field.

At the end of the day, we proudly look around at our accomplishment. Hands on our hips, we nod in satisfaction. Coke Bottle, Gimp, and I grab the handles of our chalk machines and roll back to the school.

Throughout the morning of the next day, I wander all over the playground, checking on the competitions, becoming more and more flustered to see my chalk genius being stomped and smeared by fools who cannot seem to run inside the lines. I'm a mess by the noon break.

After lunch, everyone is gathered for the announcement of when we run in the 100 yard dash. I'm confused. Did the Principal say "everyone"? I wonder if that includes me.

I check the master chart and am shocked to see I am actually scheduled to run. This is insane: I can't sprint with arch supports in my runners. Worse yet, I don't own gym shorts or a sweat shirt — I am wearing my snap-front H.A.S.H. blue jeans and tight blue Estes Rockets t-shirt. I stand there, fuming at the irresponsibility of the teachers not to tell us to wear gym clothes to Track & Field Day.

Everyone is ordered to be at their designated lane at exactly the correct time or face severe detention after school. At my scheduled time, I am on the starting line in the middle of a row of eight kids. They are doing all sorts of weird stretches. I'm bent down trying to tuck my laces into my two-stripe North Star runners, fearing I'll trip on them and look like a fool.

"On your mark!"

Everyone gets ready.

"Get set!"

I feel the top metal snap on my jeans biting into me, so I undo it.

The starting pistol bangs and we're off. I'm running as fast as I can. With my wide-legged jeans flapping back and forth, I wonder if the girls think I look like a cool blue Gumby. In a flash, all of my snaps undo, my pants slide down my hips, and I tumble to my knees.

This was before the days of everyone at least getting a participation ribbon.

Chapter 15: My Life to 1974

In the final days of Grade Eight, we receive the school assignment to each write our own short autobiographies, which I now find to be a brilliant idea for a teacher to give to thirteen year olds. Though none of it was written to be funny, I now find nearly every sentence secretly filled with dark humour. (I received a B+ for this.)

I was born on a humid Saturday morning at 5am in Shaunavon Union Hospital. My first house was on main street in Dollard Sask. It was an old unpainted shack with a high fence. In the front part of the house my mom ran the town post office.

At 1 month old I went for my first car ride in an old Chev that was pulling all our belongings in an old trailer to Regina to stay. We moved in with my uncle, aunt, and their family.

My mom was on welfare.

We moved to a yellow house and lived in the back half of it. We had running water but no sewers so we had to throw the water outside. We moved to Greer Court projects but the whole place was just mud and dirt with only 9 blocks of apartment built when we got there. There was only 3 trees there, just later they chopped down two because they were dead.

When I was 6, I remember playing in a mud puddle while it was raining. I glanced up and saw Batman — my hero at the time. I ran inside and told my mom about it and then she showed me, it was only the mailman in his raincoat with his empty mailbag.

Then I started going to school. In grade one my teacher was Sister Margaret. Everyone hated her because she always gave everyone the strap with a plastic ruler. Luckily it was plastic and usually always broke, until some stupid idiot bought her a metal one.

My first pet was a fuzzy male golden labrador pup. The next year it broke its leg and we had to put it to sleep because we couldn't afford the vet bill.

In March 1973, I entered in the Regina Science Fair and won 4th prize. It was on flatworms.

This September I'll be going to Miller High School where I'll be going for grade 9, and maybe on to grade 10, 11, and 12.

PART THREE: CHURCH

Chapter 16: Jesus Christ in our Gym

Our first real house in Regina is a little shack a few blocks away from the closest Catholic elementary school, named after Saint Augustine of Hippo.

Hippo was a city in ancient Algeria where Augustine came from. A place called Hippo is no reason to laugh. To laugh at a Saint's birthplace is reason to be slapped with the ruler. Only Protestants would make fun of a city called Hippo.

Louis and Yvette attend St. Augustine for their final elementary school years, Ape for both of his Grade Ones.

Sharing the same grounds as St. Augustine School is our church, named after Saint Thérèse of Lisieux, France. She is known as the Little Flower and that is what the beautiful church is called.

Inside it, I will soon be taught about a nice old man with a big beard called God, a nice young man with blonde hair named Jesus, and a white dove with the cool name of The Holy Ghost — sadly later changed to The Holy Spirit.

Through many childhood years of learning the Catechism, I will be told why I received Original Sin at birth, plus everything I need to memorize about Heaven, Hell, Purgatory, Eden, Moses, Noah, the Disciples (including the bad dark one), the Virgin Mary, the Crucifixion, evil Romans and Jews, heathen Protestants, bad bathroom sounds, the genesis of the world, touching oneself, sperm in Limbo, the destruction of the world, slaves (good and bad), a couple hundred Popes, Latin, how to do an emergency baptism, bastard babies, corporal punishment, the many classes of angels, King Herod (bad), King David (good), a talking snake (cool, but bad), picking a Confirmation name, why a nun wears a wedding ring, Ash Wednesday, Confession, reciting the Rosary, walking on water, and the story my sister loves: Jesus turning water into wine at a wedding, his first miracle.

While living in the little yellow house on Arcola, my whole family gets dressed-up every Sunday morning and we walk the few blocks to Mass. Dressed-up means beautiful dresses for my mom and sister, suit jackets and pants for us boys — all sewn from scratch by Mom, the master seamstress.

Though tiny Little Flower Parish was established in 1930, we are privileged to attend the gigantic, new church, built only eight years ago in 1956. (By the early 1950s, there were five Masses every Sunday — all overflowing — so a fundraising drive was started to build a much bigger church.)

I marvel at the majesty of this building, the entrance angled diagonally on the corner of College Avenue and Edgar Street. Every time, as I am about to enter, I stare up at the steeple in the clouds and trip over my feet.

Inside I am surrounded by four enormous stained-glass walls, filled with endless ideas to fuel my daydreams for the next hour: doves, flames, crowns, serpents, gold houses, a burning bush, a human heart pierced with an arrow.

I am four when we move away to a new neighbourhood a few miles away. But we still maintain our connection with Little

Flower, making our way there every Sunday until a satellite church of Little Flower Parish is set up here in our new neighbourhood.

This instant church springs to life every Sunday morning in the gymnasium of my own elementary school of St. Thomas. Here, under basketball hoops, I learn even more about God.

Problem is, surviving Mass here in the generic, boring gym is painful: an hour sitting on a hard wooden chair with nothing to look at. No stained glass vistas, no choir, no statues with exposed hearts, no kneelers for me to be in charge of putting down or up at the right time. Only two long columns of chairs and the little altar in an otherwise empty school gymnasium.

I am privy to information obtained from a reliable source that the altar is on wheels and is rolled out when the Priest and altar boys secretly set up the temporary sanctuary an hour before Mass starts. The pews (wooden school chairs) are set up on the gym floor the night before by lay people.

The altar cloth, gold chalice, plate, linen, red candle, regular candles, and ringers are kept in a compartment in the portable altar. I am guessing the wine and bread are brought in each morning fresh from the main church. Unlike most other Catholic altars, this altar-on-wheels is not made of stone or marble and contains no relics of a martyr, not even one piece of bone of an ordinary Saint.

We are taught that whenever the special red candle —the sanctuary lamp— is burning in a church, even in a temporary church like ours, it indicates the presence of Jesus Christ. My reliable source tells me the Priest has to recite a quick prayer before the candle can be properly extinguished after Mass is over, and only after all the parishioners are gone. The flame is never ever blown out with your breath. To do so is a sin, with very bad consequences. The sanctuary lamp can only be extinguished with a special Catholic candle snuffer.

I don't know why, but I make the horrible mistake of telling all this to Ape. He instantly has a demonic look in his eyes. (I still get chills with memories of that look.)

The following Sunday when we are sitting bored on our wooden chairs during the gym Mass, Ape leans over to me: "I'm gonna blow out that candle, make fucken Christ pop up!"

My body temperature plummets and I cannot move. Oh my God, the worst thing in the history of the world is about to happen and I am paralysed. Oh my God, if Ape makes Christ appear in our gym, we are in so much trouble I can't imagine. Mom will be so angry and sad. We will have to move again. Please please please make someone stop him.

There is a ruckus in the back and when I turn, Ape is no longer beside me. Several men have him in arm and neck holds, and are getting him outside. I have tears of relief.

Chapter 17: First Confession Error

First Communion is a wonderful pageant of pomp and circumstance: the girls in their best pure-white dresses, complete with veils to show modesty; us boys in crisp white shirts, black pants, clip-on little bowties or regular ties.

I have never seen my class-mates in this light before. Everyone looks pretty sharp. Mouldy Susan does not look mouldy; Patsy the Flea has no fleas; Mute looks like he is smiling; even Mean Dean looks quite dapper with his fists unclenched.

We march alphabetically down the main aisle of the massive Little Flower Church — girls in one column, boys right beside. Everyone is looking at us, the stars of the show.

When the As to Fs receive Communion and start to leave, it is now time for us Gs to Ns to kneel in our designated, rehearsed spots at the chancel, hands in prayer as we await.

"Don't chew the Eucharist," I keep repeating to myself— that's a sin—just let it dissolve on the tongue naturally.

"Never ever touch it," we are told.

"Touching the body of Christ with a finger will fill your mouth with blood, pouring out all of your blood, filling the entire church with blood and drowning all of your family and friends."

I must not do this I tell myself. Mom would be so mad and sad if I do.

(The photo on the front cover of this book is taken soon after my First Communion ceremony. It is taken downstairs in the basement of Little Flower Church, with Sister Margaret holding me, my terrified eyes asking why my mom is giving me away.)

A short while after First Communion, our Catechism starts to prepare us for Confession, our third Catholic Sacrament (after Baptism and First Communion.) This is something that sounds exciting.

I am looking forward to finally going in one of Little Flower's beautiful wood Confessionals. All I know of them is their outside, covered with intricate carvings. My sister tells me of their stuffy warmth when you close the door and are kneeling, waiting alone in the dark. You can hear murmurings but everything is thick-wood muffled. It is very peaceful, she says.

Suddenly, in the dark, you hear a panel slide open and the ritual of Confession begins. Yvette says it is a wonderful experience; therefore, it must be.

You start with: "In the name of the Father, and of the Son, and of the Holy Ghost. My last confession was [x] weeks ago. These are my sins."

You then simply list your sins, starting with your mortal sins of murder, rape, incest, adultery, theft, and false witness, then continue on to your venial sins of swearing, telling white lies, not being nice to your mom.

The best part is, no matter what you confess, everything is erased for another week. All of your sins — poof! gone, totally forgiven. I bet the Protestants are kicking themselves for not inventing this.

In Catechism class, when we are all fully prepped and excited for First Confession, Sister Margaret drops an awful bombshell, something I never thought would happen: our next sacrament will not happen at the majestic Little Flower Church but right here in our school gymnasium.

"That makes no sense, Sister!" (I say that in my head, not out loud —a venial sin nonetheless.)

I plead with Mom at the dinner table that there must be some mistake: there are no beautiful wooden Confessionals at my school. Mom is my highest authority so it always unnerves me when she defers to the wisdom of the nuns and priests. I suppose they will simply transport those big Confessionals from the church here to St. Thomas School for this epic event.

All of us penitents are happily vibrating in our wooden chairs in the gym, waiting for our turn at this Life Event. We all have our confessional cards in our hands, ready to recite the moment we enter the Confessional. My card has already started to dissolve in my nervous sweat.

Darryl G next to me gets up and walks away. I am next. A few moments later, I stand up and walk to my destiny.

I exit the gym, turn down the hallway, and am confused when a Sister points me towards the gym equipment room. I stop dead, not knowing where to go, certainly not into that room. I am firmly pointed again into the room and I obey.

I enter and see the Priest sitting on a chair, a prie-dieu

(portable wooden kneeler) before him. To his left in this very narrow room are hula-hoops and floor hockey nets and climbing ropes; to his right, boxes of volleyballs and basketballs and softballs and the port-a-pit. I kneel on the prie-dieu and he hands me a new confessional card.

"In the name of the Father and of the Son and of the Holy Ghost. This is my First Confession. These are my sins ..."

I go blank; absolutely dumb. The Priest asks me to state my sins. Holy Christ, I don't think I have any.

"David G, state your sins," he demands in a pleasant but hurry-up-there-are-people-waiting sort of way.

In a sweaty panic, I blurt out: "I beat up a kid" and am given three Hail Marys and one Our Father.

I leave the room teary-eyed and terrified —not because it wasn't the spiritual experience I thought it was going to be, but I committed a sin in my very first confession.

Lying to a Priest in a Confessional — it doesn't get any worse than that.

Well, it does. Afterwards, as I am doing my penance, I zip through Our Father and as I start my first Hail Mary, Ape's obscene version pops in my head:

Hail Mary, full of grace,
Pull down your pants and sit on my —

Chapter 18: Get into Heaven Free

On special occasions, Sister Margaret and the other nuns hand out beautifully artistic Holy Cards which portray a wide variety of Catholic images. Holy Cards have been in existence since the 15th Century, first appearing as images on woodcut parchments, and now in the 1960s, on card-stock the size of a playing card.

Some of the lesser Holy Cards are given out willy-nilly to anyone, even to Ape. These are the prayer cards with one of the dull Disciples, such as Andrew or Philip, or one of the ten-thousand saints which I have to look up in our Big Book of Catholic Saints.

I collect Holy Cards like other kids collect sports or comic book trading cards. I am so pleased to receive St. Joseph of Cupertino, the patron saint of astronauts and pilots. Though he lived in the 1600s, he later became this patron saint because he was known to levitate whenever he went into his frequent catatonic trances. Strangely, in all my time with NASA during the moon missions, I never heard any astronaut pray to St. Joseph of Cupertino.

A notch above all of these Holy Cards are the most glamorous and sought-after cards—the collector ones—that depict the Virgin Mary, the Mother of God, or the Crucifixion or a top Disciple or a cool Saint. These can only be earned with a series of extra-good deeds. The most revered one is the Heaven Card and that is the one Sister Margaret is now offering to anyone who takes Communion and goes to

Confession every Sunday for nine straight weeks. This is my goal.

When I tell Yvette of my quest, she says it's a great idea to own a Get-into-Heaven-for-Free card as you'll never know when you'll need it. (I am annoyed and slightly scared when my sister is not taking this as serious as she should, especially when she asks if I can get an extra one for her.)

Of course I am successful in earning the Heaven Card after my nine Sundays of Mass, Communion, and Confession. As a super surprise double-bonus, I also get Holy Cards with Pope John XXIII and Pope Paul VI. How lucky can a boy get?

And those are the last Holy Cards I ever receive. Though I am now on my sixth Pope—from John, Paul, the two John Pauls, Benedict, to Francis—I only have cards for the first two.

Yvette has forever stuck a blasphemous meme in my head, one that pops every time I hear any Pope's name. I always hear her voice reciting the list of Popes in a deep, exaggerated sports announcer voice yelling out the name of each football player as he runs on the field.

"And here comes number TWENTY-THREE, Johnnie two three ... followed by number SIX - Paul the man Paul. Out next together are the Johnnie-Paul twins, number ONE and number TWO, the Polish Prince."

I am sure she would have continued to the present day with, "Limping onto the field is number SIXTEEN Benedict the Quitter, and pushing him right along is the smiley new guy from Argentina. Let's hear it for Francis NO NUMBER

Frankie Frank!!!"

John XXIII has been Pope for a couple of years when I enter the world in 1960. He is said to have been elected on the eleventh ballot as a temporary pope until a more universal one can be found, but he shocks the Catholic world in 1962 with his good-god holy-shit surprise announcement of a revolutionary new Ecumenical Council: the complete modernization of the entire Roman Catholic Church known as Vatican II. "Open the windows of the Church and let in some fresh air," he says.

Traditionalists are shocked beyond belief. Extreme traditionalists tar him a heretic of modernism and refuse to accept him as the legitimate Pope. Many to this day say the Chair of Peter has been vacant since the 1958 death of Pope Pius XII and everyone elected in the decades since are all Antipopes.

This is why I love love love The One True Church: two thousand years of wealth, power, politics, drama, death — all in the name of the Catholic version of the invisible man in the sky. All swirling around a succession of two hundred and sixty six Popes—not including the forty antipopes and trickster Pope Joan—and all appointed by a dove called The Holy Ghost.

The voting procedure to elect a new Pope is quite simple. We are taught the Holy Ghost, in its form as a white dove, flies down from Heaven and enters the sealed Sistine Chapel (down the chimney, I'm guessing) during the Conclave to touch the forehead of each Cardinal with the name of the person God wants to be the next Pope. The result is always unanimous on the first ballot, every time.

To get the huge crowd in St. Peter's Square revved up, they pretend there are multiple ballots — the faithful staring up at the chimney to see if the smoke of the burned ballots is dark (non-conclusive) or white ("We have a Pope.") Though the vote is always unanimous on the first ballot every time for 2000 years, every Pope's election pretends to be recorded on how many series of ballots are made, cleverly drawing out the tension and drama. Show biz ratings are built into the Catholic Church. And more time to sell papal souvenirs in the gift shop.

The fantasy world of Lord of the Rings and countless other literary cults do not even come close to this real-life, real-people world of intrigue that has endured for twenty centuries and is truly believed by billions and billions of people.

But not me. And this is what confuses me. Why have I always been so fascinated with the many Biblical stories without them ever clicking in my head as being faith or belief? This is my life's big question mark.

Chapter 19: Vatican II

Though Pope John XXIII starts Vatican II in 1962, God decides to torture him to death with painful stomach cancer before it is finished. Seems an odd decision in my mind. The traditionalists have a temporary celebration until they are shocked to realize the new pope they elect is going to carry on exactly where the dead one left off.

Once the multitude of sessions conclude three years later in 1965, the decisions of the Second Vatican Council are sent out to every church in the Catholic world. Little did the new Pope, the Cardinals, and the many people in all of the commissions consider how this would effect me, a child on the flatlands of Canada.

Mom introduces me to the Catholic Church when I am a small child in the early-1960s, before the radical reforms from Rome trickle down to our church in Regina.

I first see the magnificent altar against the far wall, the priest always facing away from us, blocking our view of his transubstantiation magic trick. After Vatican II, it is a free-standing altar, the priest flipped around, facing the audience.

Mass was in Latin. Now it's celebrated in English words we pretend we understand. Instead of painful organ music, there is now folk music played by hippies on guitars. Nuns are free to shed their full body and head-covering gothic garb to wear modest dresses. (Sister Margaret does not change.)

In one of the many final decrees of the Council, it is affirmed that Christ intended only "one true Church." This Church of Christ uniquely 'subsists in' the Catholic Church, though it does recognize that other churches do contain some elements of truth. I think it is quite honourable and conciliatory to admit the Protestants are not completely wrong about everything. Still going to Hell, but with a little pat on the back from us.

Vatican II also started to work on the issue of the billions of unbaptized babies being tortured forever in Limbo, but they decided to shelve the topic to give the Church more time to consider. Perhaps at the next Council in one hundred years, these screaming souls will be freed.

The most shocking and terrifying change for me is accepting the Host during Mass. We were taught that physically touching a blessed Communion wafer with anything but one's tongue will send you to the blood-filled Hell of the Damned. Suddenly, as we enter the new school year after the wonderful care-free summer vacation of 1967, us kids can now accept Christ's body in our palms in September. I may have shit my pants in terror the first time.

Chapter 20: Holy Card II

I only go to one summer camp in my life and I love the first day of it: the outdoor breakfast of bacon and eggs, the hike around Katepwa Lake, the afternoon crafts of woodworking and pottery. I make a crucifix with burnt wooden matches glued to purple velvet for Mom and another clay ashtray for Yvette.

I love the evening storytelling around the campfire — great blood-curdling Bible stories, made ever-more scary being told outside at night, the campfire flames flickering up to reflect eerie faces of Protestants in the bushes.

This fun comes to an end in the afternoon of the second day when we are all ordered to put on our swim trunks, sit on the beach, and face the pier. I am stunned to learn it is swimming evaluation day and we are all being tested to see where we fit in the levels of swimming lessons to be held throughout the week.

Standing on the pier with clipboards in hand, the counsellors yell out a name and each boy walks alone down the pier. I lean forward to hear what they say to each kid, but cannot make it out. After being asked or told something, the kid either dives gracefully into the lake, slicing the water with barely a ripple, or jumps in with a loud splash and starts to tread water. The counsellors write some notes as the boy swims to shore.

I put up my hand—thinking it best to inform the camp counsellors that I have zero swimming skills and my time will be better spent in the Crafts Hut glazing my sister's ashtray—but I am ignored.

When my name is called, I walk the pier, and am told to jump in the lake.

"I can't swim," I announce to these giant men.

"Jump in, tread water. Now!"

I am speechless they do not understand my clear explanation, so I just shake my head. One counsellor points back at the beach, puts his face in mine, and yells, "Go back to your blanket and don't move until we get you!"

What seems like hours later, there are about a dozen of us boys sitting scattered on the beach, each alone facing the pier, when we are ordered to our tents to get fully dressed—long pants and long sleeves—and report to the Crafts Hut.

This is great news as I have had time to finally make a decision on what colours to paint my sister's artwork. Problem is, the Crafts Hut is locked when us outcasts start to gather there and are horrified to see the camp priest walking towards us.

Holy crap, I'm scared. How was I to know not being able to swim was a sin? I rack my brain trying to think of anything in our Catechism that is pro-swimming. All I can think of is Jesus walking on water while Peter plopped and had to be saved.

For the sin of being non-swimmers, we are sentenced to walk back-and-forth down the dusty grid road in the summer heat to a mountain of bricks that have been dumped by the camp gate and carry all back to camp. This we do each day during the time the others are having their swimming lessons. We are told we are doing God's work as these donated bricks will be used to build the new outdoor chapel.

The priest does not tell us we are earning Holy Cards by doing this work, but, back home, Yvette assures me that I definitely, absolutely earned another Heaven Card. I believe everything my sister says.

Chapter 21: No Saint Bob

Quickly after I was born, I receive the first Catholic sacrament of Baptism, then when I enter school years later, I get two more: Communion and Confession. Now I am going for Sacrament #4: Confirmation.

The most fantastical part of Confirmation is we get another name and as far as I know, I am the only kid whose mom is allowing him to pick his own Confirmation name. All my friends have had theirs chosen for them. My mom is the coolest.

It is made a little challenging as the name must be one of the many Catholic Saints. I am thinking of some of my favourite astronauts but cannot find a Saint Gus or a Saint Neil in our Big Book of Saints.

My sister loves Bob Dylan and is pushing me to choose Bob.

"There's no Saint Bob, Yvette! It has to be a Saint."

She insists there must be a Saint Bob but I cannot find one.

Ape tries to help by suggesting Saint Stupid Shit-head.

(Much later I find out there is a Catholic Saint Bob, but I know I would have rejected taking St. Robert Bellarmine's name as he is the buffoon who ordered Galileo to renounce the theory of the Earth orbiting the Sun.)

You can only get the Big Three Cs of Communion, Confession, and Confirmation once you have reached what Catholics call The Age of Discretion, which is around seven years old. This is the age when we become capable of making free acts of the will and therefore morally responsible for our actions. Before seven, if you do something really bad, it will be completely forgiven. After your seventh birthday, you're doomed to Hell.

Sadly, I only find out about this total amnesty rule when I am much older. If I had known before I turned seven, I wonder if I would have hesitated as much as I did before my chemistry-set experiment of potassium chloride in Ape's milk.

The only challenge with my upcoming Confirmation is finding a male Sponsor and that is a damn hard task living in the Greer Court projects filled with many single moms and very few adult males. To be a Sponsor, the nabbed man has to be a practicing Catholic who has received the four sacraments and, more importantly, is not a public sinner.

I am so happy when Mom tells me that she has convinced Mr. S to be my Sponsor. He is the dad of Paul, a friend of mine, one of the few people I know who has a father.

To honour my friend, I first consider my Confirmation Name to be Paul (a damn good choice I must say,) but must change it as it is Ape's middle name. Instead, I choose Patrick, the name of another friend.

Weeks later, in a lavish ceremony equal to my First Communion, Mom proudly watches as the Archbishop anoints my forehead in the shape of a cross with chrism (blessed olive oil and balm) then gives my face a symbolic slap.

I am now officially confirmed, am announced as Alfred David Patrick G, and am forever a member of the Roman

Catholic Church.

And I'm not joking about "forever."

It is truly impossible to become a non-Catholic once you are one.

No matter what you say or do, you cannot get out of this club.

You can't even quit.

The moment I received the Catholic sacraments of Baptism, Communion, Confession, and Confirmation, I am considered a member in *saecula saeculorum* (forever AND ever.) If I honestly state my non-belief in the events and characters in the Bible, it does not matter.

Not believing in God and Jesus, which you would think would be the basic prerequisite, does not get me barred.

I am classified as a "fallen" Catholic or a "lapsed" one, but still considered a Catholic. If I join any Christian-killing terrorist group, I will simply be called "a bad Catholic."

Even if I say or do something blasphemous and get excommunicated by the Pope himself, that only means I cannot temporarily partake in Communion or other Church activities until I repent.

The One True Church will never rip up my Holy Cards. She has complete confidence I will one day come crawling back.

Chapter 22: My First Drink of Blood

Our church's Priest, Father Holler, is going to celebrate a full Mass in our Grade Seven school classroom in St. Thomas. All the desks have been pushed against every wall and an impromptu altar has been built by the blackboard. For Communion, we are surprised and thrilled he has brought the golden chalice from the main Church and announces we will drink from it.

Communion for us has always been a thin, bone-dry white wafer on our tongue and nothing else. Today is a good day as we are getting grape juice to wash it down.

And this event is made even more exciting as we are finally going to have a closeup view of transubstantiation happen right before our eyes: the actual conversion of the wafer and juice into Christ's body and blood. Not just symbolically, but literally. The Priest does this during every Mass, but he is usually far away, up there behind the altar, so we have never really seen how it is done.

Not believing in transubstantiation was one reason that Luther guy was excommunicated five hundred years ago. Simply because he would not accept this mysterious process that truly surpasses understanding.

We all watch spellbound as Father Holler prepares Communion, but it is looking and sounding the same as it always does.

"Take this, all of you, and eat of it: for this is my body which will be given up for you."

"Take this, all of you, and drink from it: for this is the chalice of my blood, the blood of the new and eternal covenant, which will be poured out for you and for many for the forgiveness of sins. Do this in memory of me."

Father Holler lifts the chalice and boom — it's done.

I didn't see it; I don't get it.

I must have blinked because I missed the big moment. The wafer and juice was just transformed into Christ's body and blood and I miss it? How stupid am I?

Lined up in our classroom to receive Communion — girls in one column, their elbows slightly softly touching us boys right beside — Father Holler starts to put the body of Christ on each of our tongues then offering a drink from the gold chalice.

I hear him say, "The body and blood of Christ," followed by a child's "Amen."

"The body and blood of Christ." "Amen."

"The body and blood of Christ." "Amen."

This, of course, is happening alphabetically and I am impatiently waiting back in the Gs, in disbelief that in a few moments I am going to taste the blood of Christ.

"The body and blood of Christ." "Amen."

"The body and blood of Christ." "Amen."

The kid in front of me moves away and now it's my turn.

"The body and blood of Christ."

I say my Amen, accept the host on my tongue, then grab

ahold of the large gold chalice and tip it for a sip. A drizzle of strong-tasting juice fills my mouth and I choke a bit, abruptly lowering the chalice. A dribble of blood drips off my chin onto my shirt.

That's not the Welch's that Mom buys. Father is smiling as I hand it back to him.

I quickly turn to go back to my place on the far side of the classroom. I feel funny. My stomach is hot. I don't know why I'm blinking so much. I look around to the other communicants and everyone else is eerily silent, many red-faced, some swaying in place.

Receiving Christ's blood for the first time is a powerful spiritual event in our young lives.

Chapter 23: Limbo and Playing with Yourself

Father Holler is also called into our classroom to instruct us boys not to play with ourselves, a wonderful phrase for this horrific sin, lest the spilled sperm—those unfortunate, sad half-souls—slide down to Limbo for an eternity of aching.

We learn the other half of the soul, the egg inside the virginal female, is waiting to be matched by God to its specific counterpart sperm. This can only happen with a husband and wife in a darkened bedroom.

One sperm and one egg creates one Catholic human being:

this makes perfect sense.

I wish my child brain would have stopped there, with no more wondering about certain details. (Ideally, religious instruction should not lead to any form of thinking.) The reason for my new distress is my numbers do not add up: the shocking difference in numbers of sperm vis-a-vis eggs. Many million sperm, each with a half-soul, swim furiously towards its one half-soul egg counterpart?

According to my sister's high school biology books and our set of Family Health encyclopaedia (with the cool semi-transparent pages of all the body organs, especially boobs), I learn that a girl's body will only release a few hundred eggs in her entire lifetime.

Let's say, in a given month, a boy releases ten million sperm once a day after school—hypothetically speaking, of course—while, that same month, his dream girl will only release one egg into her womb. Even if they got together in real life, one day after school, only one of his millions of half-souls will ever match up with her one half-soul.

The discrepancy is astronomical. My brain and body hurts from thinking about all the unmatched halves swimming blindly. I am open to the idea I may have misinterpreted something along the way, but I need to verify the divine mystery of why one plus one equals one.

In Catechism we are taught about the four places where souls are divided into after death: Heaven, Hell of the Damned (shortened to Hell), Purgatory, and Limbo.

Heaven and Hell are self-explanatory, though I must say I prefer staring at the blood-red paintings of horrific Hell over the dull, light-blue ones of fluffy Heaven. I know Heaven is the place we must all attain, but, quite frankly, what Sister Margaret describes seems terribly boring.

I imagine an eternity of sitting at Grandma's kitchen table at the farmhouse, sitting straight, no talking, no feet wiggling, no music, just the sound of the clock.

Hell is an eternity of pain, suffering, and hurt. The good part, unlike quiet Heaven, loud Hell will have lots of poking and prodding, plus many other things to keep you busy forever. Cigarette smoking is allowed everywhere so that's a little bit of good news for those life-long smokers. And the perpetual open bar helps too.

Purgatory is simply Heaven's Waiting Room, just one last check to see if your soul is in order before you are sent up the stairs.

I do not know how long you wait there, or if there are chairs or National Geographics. The word Purgatory means "to make clean" and is a place where departed souls exist because they left their human bodies in God's grace but not entirely free from venial fault. Their debt must be cleansed by suffering before their admission to Heaven.

I can see how this might happen. Let's say I am walking down the street and am hit and killed by a bus or a meteorite. I obviously would not have had time for a Last Confession and would leave this world with a few undissolved sins.

One month after my Grandma's funeral, we travel back to Ponteix for a special Mass in her honour, to help boost her into Heaven in the off-chance she is stuck in Purgatory.

But as far as I know, Grandma was conscious when she was dying in the Swift Current hospital and most likely had her final Confession. A priest also would have performed the seventh sacrament, Extreme Unction (more commonly called Last Rites.)

I don't get it. Did she do or think something immediately before she died that we have to double-check to make sure it has been wiped clean?

Limbo is quite complicated and the entrance requirements are quite varied. In Latin it is *limbus*, meaning edge or boundary, and though technically located in Hell, it is not in the bad part of it. Limbo is like that cool artsy little neighbourhood that is in the bad area of your town.

Limbo is divided into two sections. The old section, now devoid of souls, is just a big empty dusty room with garbage scattered all over the floor. This part is called Limbo of the Patriarchs (Latin: *limbus patrum*) and it is where every good person from the beginning of time waited until Christ Himself dies on the cross in 33 A.D.

That is a lot of people, and includes all the big names from the Old Testament: Moses, Noah, Abraham. They were forbidden to enter Heaven because of the sin of Adam and their punishment was to wait until Christ arrives with their tickets. Some of them wait a heck of a long time.

I am guessing the person who waited the shortest was The Good Thief, the one crucified beside Christ. He must have barely had time to get a drink and start to mingle before hearing the announcement to move upstairs.

Though they were somewhat pissed they had to wait all that time, some for a few centuries, everyone is honoured Christ goes out of his way to get them. When someone goes down to Hell to save you—literally, like he did—you'll be forever grateful.

The other section of Limbo is called Limbo of Infants (Latin: *limbus infantium*) and is overflowing with screaming babies who died without receiving Catholic Baptism.

Though they died without any personal mortal sin, they did die with Original Sin and for that reason they must be confined and punished forever.

This section of Limbo has no time limit, or seating capacity of any kind, and must be bursting at the seams. My anxiety escalates just thinking of the immense and ever-growing crowd of souls in this part of Limbo.

The sad part is these babies are not going to be rescued one day. They are here forever because they died before their Original Sin could be washed away with Baptism. God, that makes me sad.

I am very happy the day we are taught how to do an emergency Baptism. With this knowledge, I will be able to send many babies to Heaven. Yvette says I should not say that out loud but I don't see why not.

If we are ever babysitting a baby and it starts to die, we are to immediately pour water on its head and say a prayer, preferably Our Father. That way, if the baby dies, it will go to directly to Heaven not Limbo.

I am supposing the first thing we do after the emergency Baptism is to yell for help.

One of my classmates puts up her hand to ask if it has to be holy water. The answer is no. The act of prayer will make the tap water holy. Another asks if 7Up can be used. A snap of knuckles to the forehead is the answer to that kid's question.

As I see him dragged off to Detention, I shake my head at the stupidity of some of my classmates on these matters of important religious dogma.

All this does not solve my soul number issue: all of my half-souls constantly sliding down into Limbo, knocking about all the screaming babies.

And since my vasectomy at age twenty-five, what has been happening to the countless number of sperm my body has created then dissolved into itself? I really hope there are not trillions of half-souls in my pants.

Chapter 24: Can't Hold a Candle

I love my Catholic Catechism classes, probably more than everyone else in my class. Mom proudly supports my two childhood obsessions: the Catechism and the Apollo moon missions. Both are full of great stories of adventure.

I consider every religion to be absolutely equal in its own fantasy. Well, except for Christianity: no other can hold a candle to the incredible stories in the Christian Bible.

That is a bold statement as I love to read the supernatural phenomena of all of the world's beliefs, big and small, single or multi-god, current or extinct. The more I study, the more it quickens my quest to find out why people believe and why I never do — not for a moment, not even once in my childhood. I still try to trick myself into believing but that never works.

There are many thrilling Jesus stories. My sister's favourite is his very first miracle when he magically changes water into wine. I can still hear her voice: "Now THAT'S a guy to hang out with."

For the heathen fornicators who do not know the story: Jesus is hanging out with his disciples at a wedding when, well, I will quote directly from the Bible, Gospel of John, Chapter 2:

[3] When the wine ran short, the mother of Jesus said to him, "They have no wine."

[4] And Jesus said to her, "Woman, how does your concern affect me? My hour has not yet come."

[5] His mother said to the servers, "Do whatever he

tells you."

[6] Now there were six stone water jars there for Jewish ceremonial washings, each holding twenty to thirty gallons.

[7] Jesus told them, "Fill the jars with water." So they filled them to the brim.

[8] Then he told them, "Draw some out now and take it to the headwaiter." So they took it.

[9] And when the headwaiter tasted the water that had become wine, without knowing where it came from (although the servers who had drawn the water knew), the headwaiter called the bride-groom and said to him,

[10] "Everyone serves good wine first, and then when people have drunk freely, an inferior one; but you have kept the good wine until now."

[11] Jesus did this as the beginning of his signs in Cana in Galilee and so revealed his glory, and his disciples began to believe in him.

First off, I cannot believe Jesus calls his own mother "Woman" in front of his friends. It would not have ended well if my mom had ever asked me to do an errand and I had answered, "Woman, how does your concern affect me? My hour has not yet come."

And I love Verse 11 quoted above. The disciples of Jesus only "began to believe in him" after first-hand witnessing him turn water into wine. Hell ya, that would be my turning point too.

In Catechism class, I absolutely love drawing the many Biblical stories with my eight-pack of super colour Crayolas: Noah and the ark, the birth of baby Jesus in the manger, Doubting Thomas thrusting his finger into Christ's side.

I will always remember looking around the Catechism classroom and not seeing everyone as excited as I am. "These are incredible stories!" I want to tell these dullards, better than Thunderbirds or Batman.

How can you resist the wonderful story of The Flood? God goes mental and plans to destroy the whole world. He gives a heads-up to Noah to build a weatherproof boat big enough to fit himself, his wife, his three sons, their three wives, and every animal and bird. A pretty big task for a five-hundred-year-old man, but he does it.

The rain starts and everyone on Earth drowns. And not just the evil people who ticked God off; devout followers, honest people, children, new-born babies: all dead. The Creator of the Universe killing 99.99% of all humanity and animal life is a hell of a story.

Omnipotent God could have easily twitched his nose like Samantha on Bewitched and everyone would have disappeared and he could start his human project fresh, but that would be awfully boring. It is a much greater visual to have millions of bloated human and animal corpses bobbing on the new worldwide ocean.

In Genesis chapter 9, to soothe ruffled feathers, God

promises to never ever again drown everyone in the world:

> [14] When I bring clouds over the earth, and the
> bow appears in the clouds,
> [15] I will recall the covenant I have made between
> me and you and all living beings, so that the waters
> shall never again become a flood to destroy all
> mortal beings.

God admits he is responsible for murdering everyone in the world, but ... look over there: a rainbow! And I admire how God lawyerly promises to never again drown humanity, leaving open options to kill us in other ways.

(I am annoyed when I later become aware of the many cultures from every part of the world that stole our Christian Bible flood story to use as their own: Mesopotamia, Ancient Greece, Maya, India, China. Too bad the Bible wasn't copyrighted.)

Not studying the Catechism herself but seeing my intense interest in it, my wonderful sister helps with my homework by asking me to read aloud the parts of the Bible. I am still surprised on how much time a teen girl spends with her little brother; she's the best sister in the world.

A few times she asks me to read in front of her and a few of her girlfriends. I love an audience, especially one as attentive as this one. They each have a passage already picked out for me. I ask if I can go get Mom to listen too; Yvette says absolutely not

— it's our secret class.

I lift up our family's heavy, leather-clad Bible and flip to the girls' first suggested passage: Genesis 19. I am excited about this one as I see there are angels in it. I begin reciting where two travelling angels show up outside Lot's house (yes, a funny name — don't laugh) and he invites them in for some cake and to stay the night ...

> [4] Before they went to bed, all the townsmen of Sodom, both young and old - all the people to the last man - closed in on the house.
> [5] They called to Lot and said to him, "Where are the men who came to your house tonight? Bring them out to us that we may have intimacies with them."
> [6] Lot went out to meet them at the entrance. When he had shut the door behind him,
> [7] he said, "I beg you, my brothers, not to do this wicked thing.
> [8] I have two daughters who have never had intercourse with men. Let me bring them out to you, and you may do to them as you please. But don't do anything to these men, for you know they have come under the shelter of my roof."

Yvette and her friends are laughing. I'm not sure why a story of someone protecting two angels against a violent mob produces girlie giggles.

104

"Continue on with verse 31," they snicker.

Lot is living in a cave with his two daughters when:
>   [31] The older one said to the younger: "Our father
>   is getting old, and there is not a man on earth to
>   unite with us as was the custom everywhere.
>   [32] Come, let us ply our father with wine and then
>   lie with him, that we may have offspring by our
>   father."
>   [33] So that night they plied their father with wine,
>   and the older one went in and lay with her father;
>   but he was not aware of her lying down or her
>   getting up.
>   [34] Next day the older one said to the younger:
>   "Last night it was I who lay with my father. Let us
>   ply him with wine again tonight, and then you go in
>   and lie with him, that we may both have offspring
>   by our father."
>   [35] So that night, too, they plied their father with
>   wine, and then the younger one went in and lay
>   with him; but again he was not aware of her lying
>   down or her getting up.
>   [36] Thus both of Lot's daughters became pregnant
>   by their father.

Oh, I'm so confused — Yvette and her girlfriends won't stop laughing. They beg me to read another one. I flip to Ezekiel 23 and start reading where Yvette is pointing:

105

[7] Thus she gave herself as a harlot to them, to all the elite of the Assyrians, and she defiled herself with all those for whom she lusted (with all their idols).

[8] She did not give up the harlotry which she had begun in Egypt, when they had lain with her as a young girl, fondling her virginal breasts and pouring out their impurities on her—

I drop the Bible. "Don't tell Mom!" Yvette laughs as I race out of the room. I have no idea how, but I am afraid I may have unwillingly participated in a sin. I make a point of telling this to the Priest in my next Confession.

Chapter 25: The Godfather

A couple of decades later, Yvette and her husband fly to Regina for the Catholic Baptism of their new baby. Though I am bewildered why she is doing this —her new family not Catholic in any way— I am excited to see my sister and my new little niece.

It is the morning of the Baptism and we are all getting dressed at Mom's house. Yvette had asked me to be the Godfather and I had simply said there is no way I would vow to help raise the child in the Catholic faith. Instead, she tells Ape he is going to do it. Just agree with what the Priest says. He nods his head.

I think Ape does a great job during the service:

Priest: "Do you reject Satan?"

Ape: "Yah."

"And all his works?"

"Yup."

"Do you reject sin, so as to live in the freedom of God's children?"

"Yah."

"Do you believe in God, the Father almighty, creator of heaven and earth?"

"Uh-huh."

"Do you believe in Jesus Christ, his only Son, our Lord, who was born of the Virgin Mary, was crucified, died, and was buried, rose from the dead, and is now seated at the right hand of the Father?"

"Oh ya."

"Do you believe in the Holy Spirit, the Holy Catholic Church, the communion of saints, the forgiveness of sins, the resurrection of the body, and life everlasting?"

"For sure."

This is one of the happiest days in our mother's life: seeing another generation absorbed into the Catholic Church.

Chapter 26: Catholic Loophole

As devout true Catholics cannot get divorced, Mom lists her marital status as "legally separated" for nearly fifty years. She only stops writing "Mrs." on her signature in the 1980s, though she forever retains her married name and insists it be on her gravestone. She knows she can easily get a legal, worldly divorce but it would mean nothing if she is forever married according to God and his Catholic Church.

It is not until she is updating her will when I casually mention there is a tiny possibility that Maurice could contest it, as they are still technically married. She panics — she wants all of her life assets that she earned entirely on her own to be split equally amongst her children and grandchildren and no one else. She starts divorce proceedings and is shocked how quickly it's done.

Now that she has easily severed the earthly human-law connection to her vile husband, she starts to wonder if there is something somewhere in Church rules that could retroactively dissolve their Catholic marriage itself. Her parish priest says no: God created marriage as a permanent union. When two people marry, they form an unbreakable bond. Jesus himself taught that:

> they are no longer two, but one flesh. Therefore, what God has joined together, no human being must separate." [Matthew 19:6]

For the first time in her life, she cannot accept the words of a

Catholic priest. She tells me she is often distraught to the point of physical paralysis — frozen in prayer, rosary in hand. When she tells me she cannot sleep due to never-ending nightmares of being seated next to Maurice for eternity, it makes me so upset I want to shake her.

I tell her that every marriage is null and void in Heaven. "Remember, Mom, it's only 'till death us do part.' No one's married after they die," is my feeble attempt to convince her. "Everyone's free and single again! You don't even have to sit with your own family," I joke. Mom hears nothing I say.

She starts on a frantic search and soon stumbles onto a canon law called Declaration of Nullity. Luckily, after two millennia of existence, The One True Church has a few loopholes for everything.

How can you not love a religion that has human asterisks behind every God-given rule?

This is the cool part: a Declaration of Nullity does not nullify an existing marriage. What it does is declare the wedding and marriage to NEVER have ever existed in the eyes of God and his Catholic Church — a backwards time-travel eraser. I bet the Protestants never thought of this gem.

But Mom is scared to start a matrimonial nullity trial as she will have to appear before a Church Court to prove the man she married had no intention of entering into a lifelong union when he said his wedding vows to her in 1950. And she has to provide evidence and witness statements proving he did not have the mental capacity to know what a marriage means.

She never does finalize a Declaration of Nullity before she

drops dead in her vegetable garden. I am so happy her brain death was instantaneous; if she had been aware in her final hours or days before death, it would have been a hysterical living hell for her as she awaits her fate down to the real Hell.

Because, in their eyes, she does die as an unfaithful wife, mother of a bastard baby born outside of marriage.

And what would drive her into insanity in her final moments is her lack of knowing where Maurice is. If he confessed all his sins to a priest before his death, he is now safely far away from her, lounging in Heaven. If he left the world in a state of sin, he'll be waiting for her in the Torments of Hell.

Chapter 27: Seeing My Mom's Face Again

In September 2013, a story explodes worldwide of what Pope Francis wrote in a letter to an Italian newspaper. No one can stop a sensational headline from going viral. I post it and send it to everyone I know, as did every smug atheist and every anti-Catholic Christian (not that I'm either.)

"Pope says good atheists can go to heaven"

It seems plausible. After all, he did ignite a press conference soon after he was elected Pope by answering a journalist's moral question with "Who am I to judge?"

And if atheists are allowed in Heaven, I can't wait to see my mother's face when I show up:

"David?!! What the hell are you doing here???" spilling her egg salad sandwich into her lap. (I've always thought that's what you eat in Heaven; I don't know why.)

But it was too good to be true. Pope Frankie never said anything of the sort. On the Vatican website is "Letter to a Non-believer," his full and lengthy statement saying God "forgives" non-believers, but he never goes so far to say our names will be on the guest list. The velvet rope will be unhinged for us only if we are contrite and express remorse. Then he teases us with:

> The issue for the unbeliever lies in obeying his or her conscience. There is sin, even for those who have no faith, when conscience is not followed. Listening to and obeying conscience means deciding in the face of what is understood to be good or evil. It is on the basis of this choice that the goodness or evil of our actions is determined.

I have a page from my childhood Catechism workbook where the question is to define sin. Written in my eight-year-old's bad handwriting, I explain:

> Sin is saying no to god. Sin is something that you do even when your concience tells you to do otherwise.
> It isn't a sin when you think its right but it isnt.

In angry red ink on the top of the page is my mark for this assignment: 1/5. I'm going to bring this sheet with me to Heaven and shove it in the face of the Sister who gave me the failing mark (assuming she is in Heaven.

PART FOUR: HOME

Chapter 28: Pile of Bones

I spend my entire childhood in Regina, the capital city of the rectangle province of Saskatchewan located on the flatlands of Western Canada — with its dry, scorching hot summers, brief autumns, followed by long, dark winters of face-freezing, mind-numbing, indescribable cold, then quick springtimes. Repeat.

Who lives in a place that annually goes from forty-below to forty-above? Every winter when the temperature plummets and the city stops, I shake my head at the brave refugees from around the world who escape war, persecution, and poverty to move here, only to realize if they simply stand outside for more than five minutes, their ears will fall off and they will die.

Weather is the consistent daily topic of conversation in Saskatchewan. If you are travelling through, we don't care to hear about your family or your job. All we need to know is "how's the roads?" (Men may have the follow-up question of, "what's that you're driving?")

I have heard the etymology of the name of my province is a phrase meaning, "I think I drove through it once." Yvette says Saskatchewan is derived from a First Nations word meaning "whatstheretodo." Yes, she is correct in it being a Cree word, but it is from kisiskâciwani-sîpiy, meaning "swift flowing river" (though that river is far from us.) I like my sister's version as my childhood is a constant struggle to burn time. Boredom is the dread enemy of prairie kids. We sometimes eat a big bowl of baked beans first thing in the morning just so we have something to do all day.

One of Regina's most beautiful landmarks was created by bored people: the Albert Memorial Bridge, a government work project started when the Depression hit in 1929 and there were many idle men. When Reginians show off our beautiful urban park—alongside Wascana Creek—to visitors, they always brag about this structure: "the world's longest bridge over the shortest span of water." Unfortunately, this is completely true: its 250 metre length spans the tiny twenty-five metre wide creek, 90% of the bridge structure plunked on dry land.

I brag about the beauty of the bridge, especially its glazed terra-cotta balusters — never about the absurdity of its length that no one here is embarrassed about.

Regina is called The Queen City as Regina is Latin for Queen. In 1882, Princess Louise suggests the name in honour of her mother, Queen Victoria, the reigning monarch at the time. Princess Louise, a member of the British royalty, insanely bored with her life in Ottawa as the wife of the Governor General of Canada, occupies her time by giving place-names to many locations across our new country. Not a bad hobby I must say.

Though her suggestion is accepted and the new settlement is formally named Regina in the summer of 1882, this place is not much more than a few tents and shacks. The naming is only symbolic as this empty spot on the treeless patch of dry prairie has been arbitrarily chosen to become the location for the planned Territorial capital.

And a horrible and illogical spot for a settlement.

The three other suggested locations for the new capital have abundant water sources, natural beauty, plus trees for fuel, shade, and lumber. Regina has none of these. Its only advantage is that this spot is directly in the path of the proposed transcontinental railway.

(And, by happenstance, the Territorial Lieutenant-Governor, Edgar Dewdney, had reserved substantial land on the site for himself.)

Before the British princess names it Regina, this place was known for time immemorial as oskana kâ-asastêki — "Pile of Bones."

For thousands of years, hunters followed the thunderous and inexhaustible herds of bison across the prairies, using much of the kill for food, shelter, clothing, utensils, weapons. Along the shores of the slow, meandering creek called oskana—which passes through present-day Regina—the unused bison bones are stacked in towering mounds, an incredible site to see from afar on the flatlands. Many people believe the wild herds will return to the area to visit these huge piles of bones.

Throughout my childhood, bison do return every August during Buffalo Days, Regina's week-long summer carnival and exhibition, launched each year with a big party on Pile of Bones Sunday. The cartoon mascot is Pemmican Pete: a blonde, full-bearded, tan-leather-clad man, rifle in his right hand, waving yellow hat in the other, riding bareback on a happy bison.

117

To celebrate Buffalo Days, we eat cotton candy, spin around on fun rides, get flustered in the house of mirrors, stand in line for rush tickets for the Stampeders concert.

Chapter 29: The Pinky Fire

In September 1960, my farmer father drops off the possessions of his lover and one-month-old baby in the big city, then turns around to drive back to his mother.

We move in with my uncle George and Auntie Eva (Mom's sister, two years older) who have a tiny living area behind their barber shop and beauty salon near downtown Regina.

This is where I live my first few months of life in 1960 with my mom, my three siblings, my uncle and aunt, and their three young kids.

Shortly thereafter, we move around the corner to an attic we can call our own.

In 1961, my mother's dream home comes true. We move into 417 Arcola Avenue, the back half of a one-storey wooden house on an industrial street. It is a beautiful yellow house with a white picket fence, land for a big vegetable garden, a school close by, no indoor toilet, no hot water, no adult able to stand up in the kitchen due to the sloped ceiling, everyone sleeping in two beds in one bedroom, with me in a crib until age four. Things are looking even better.

118

Once spring arrives, my mother's farm roots explode into a frenzy of vegetable gardening: carrots, potatoes, beets, lettuce, corn. I am teased as a toddler for crying when I get lost in the corn field, though it is amazing how small an area it is with adult eyes.

I have one of my best early childhood memories of total happiness and freedom living there: running giggling in the rain in the street in my rubber boots. I am such a happy and contented kid, oblivious of the horrendous living conditions of my siblings and of the unending paralyzing worry of my mother.

At bath time, with no hot water plumbing in the house, Mom heats water in big pots on our little stove then pours it into The Giant Tub. The big metal wash tub is on the kitchen floor when Ape and I take our shared baths, and in the bedroom for privacy when the others take their separate ones.

Ape and my shared baths come to a quick end when he can no longer control his laughter at every floating turd he makes. From then on, I bathe first and alone, with Ape afterwards in my bath water.

We have an electric washing machine with scary rollers that crush children's fingers. I am always at a distance when Mom is operating the loud, clanky bone-crushing rollers to squeeze out my washed diapers.

She heats water on the stove to use in the washing machine

for my clothes and other daily essentials. All of the other washing—clothes, sheets, towels—are placed in the big metal wash tub and carried to the nearby laundromat. The name is Pinky's Laundromat and I always smile when I see the pink elephant on the sign.

Early on every one of the frequent Laundry Days, my mother fills the tub with all of our items, rubbing the soiled parts with lye soap, gives Louis and Yvette the exact number of needed quarters, a container of soap, and sends them off to carry the heavy tub to the laundromat before school.

Ape is with them as well and never wants to go to school. Aside from carrying the big tub, they must grab and hold wild Ape all the way.

Louis and Yvette fill the washers, pour in the soap, plug in the valuable quarters, and try to drag their hairy little brother before the bell rings at St. Augustine School a few blocks away.

Back home, Mom is continuing her endless household tasks and getting me ready, timing her household departure so we arrive at the laundromat the moment the wash cycle is finished.

No money for the dryers, she places the damp clothes back in the giant metal tub, carries the heavy tub outside to our metal wagon (or winter sled), plops me on top, and goes home to hang the clothes on our giant back yard clothes line.

In the winter months, she has an elaborate series of cords throughout our tiny house where the damp clothes are hung; I love walking and crawling under this global canopy of fresh laundry.

With me babbling to myself in the wagon along the sidewalk

on our way to get our clothes at the laundromat, we turn the corner from Arcola Avenue onto Victoria Avenue to see the horror of horrors: the laundromat is on fire.

Mom starts running, selfishly neglecting to think of me clasping onto the sides of the wagon in fear of my life.

Lots of people are on the sidewalk when we arrive. I experience my first distinct smell of building fire. There is smoke and noise and chaos; I'm scared out of my mind.

I vaguely hear my mother's voice say something like "take care of my son" and feel my hand being held by someone. I look up to see it is being held by a strange woman.

I look for my mom and find her running into the on-fire laundromat. Why in the world has she given me away to this stranger? And even at this young age, I'm asking myself: who the hell runs into a burning building?

Many years later, my sister tries to joke about "The Pinky Fire," teasing Mom that she was a crazy woman running into a burning building to save her tea towels.

"We had no money to buy anything! We would have had nothing!" she snaps back. It is never joked about ever again.

Chapter 30: The Dagger Gang

In 1964, at my age four, my mom gets the luckiest break, the biggest boost she will ever receive in her life: her acceptance into the new public housing project on the east edge of town.

Greer Court is a newly-built 141-townhouse project of the federal government, designed for low-income people with rent based on the family's income. Without our acceptance into the project, my mother's life would have stayed awful. Worse yet, I would have grown up without hot water and could possibly still be sleeping in a crib. Moving into our new government-built townhouse with its three separate bedrooms and a living room is the momentous start of every good thing that happens in our lives.

Many times during the year prior to moving in, Mom and I walk eastward two kilometres from our little yellow house on Arcola to watch our new housing project being built near Park Street. This is such a thrill for me; I am sure she loves pulling me in the wagon along busy Victoria Avenue.

When we finally do move into our two-storey home, there is still much construction for me to supervise all around: sidewalk pouring, brick fence building, parking lot paving. Racing out the back door at full speed, I recall being in mid-air then plummeting down into a hole, suddenly remembering our back step is not yet in place.

Broken pieces of plasterboard—some people call it gyprock; the stuff every interior wall is made of—are everywhere in our construction project neighbourhood. They are, in essence, perfect pieces of chalk easily available to anyone to pick up and write something on the many sidewalks and brick walls.

The first time I see every bad word in my life, it is written in chalk. Many are horribly misspelled. It is only many years later when I discover that the proper spelling of a girl's lower parts starts with a C, not a K.

This huge housing project is ideal for us horde of kids. Greer Court is a maze of row housing among wide sidewalks for bike racing and hopscotch, low wooden fences to jump over, high brick walls to climb over, wooden garbage boxes to hide in. There are several large grassy areas to play British Bulldog, soccer, softball, and the myriad of other pickup games that result in happy laughter, squeals of fun, or everyone running home when Ape goes mental and starts pounding heads.

"We were so poor, all we had to play with were blocks of cement." Though this woe-is-me is partially true, it misses the point of how much fun this can be. Across a field to the east of the project is the concrete plant, with mountains of discarded slabs of every shape and size —free for the taking. I make many sturdy, brilliantly designed forts by myself there.

Right beside us on Park Street is the one of the most revered places on Earth, the one we run to after weekly Mass: the Coca-Cola plant. For reasons I've never discovered, the kind, generous people at the Coke plant give away little bottles to us hypnotized kids every Sunday. This got me addicted and I bought a Coke every day until I was an adult; this free giveaway in the mid-1960s had an incredible return-on-investment for those wonderful people.

Ideally situated on the southeast corner of the project is one of the main focal points of our young lives: the amazing corner store of Jim's Lucky Dollar.

"Go to Jim's and get my Craven Ms," my sister whispers to me, giving me three quarters and letting me spend the dime change. I know that I am lucky. Most other kids have to bring most or all the cigarette change back to their older siblings or mothers.

"No! Lemme go for ya!" Ape always tries to intervene whenever he overhears. Yvette never trusts him with getting her smokes.

Jim loves kids. His wife (Mrs. Jim, we call her) hates us. We never see them in the Lucky Dollar at the same time. Jim always greets us with a smile and a hello. Mrs. Jim greets us with a frown.

We unintentionally prolong her agony by taking an enormous amount of time to decide what to buy from the store-length counter of every candy in the world.

Mojos are two for a penny but deciding which ones to buy is a big task. A double-bubble is a penny each. Popeye cigarettes are five cents. A Coke is twelve. Old Dutch chips are fifteen. A purchase is not something to be entered into lightly; there are multiple methods of long-term budgeting and calculations that need to be cross-referenced first.

"Let's see ... I'd like one vanilla mojo ... ummmm ... that's half a cent ... aaaaaand — "

Mrs. Jim always explodes with, "Boy boy, buy buy! You boy -- buy! Boy buy!"

I think Mrs. Jim is a terrible salesperson.

There is a loose-knit group of kids headed by Mean Dean who roam the Greer Court neighbourhood in what might be called a gang. I hang out on its periphery, invisibly following along to see what they are up to.

I have a slight admiration for Mean Dean as he is the only person who ever picked me first for a team. A few months back, our teacher chooses Dean as one of three team leaders for a group Science Project. When they are told to start picking their team, he stands, points directly at me, and says, "I want David G." Every other scenario in the world of Dean pointing at me with those words would scare the shit out of me, but not this time. I become permanently in his good books as everyone on his team receives an A+ for the project, though it's my brilliance that puts us over the top.

Getting right into gang life, I do what any new recruit does: design a logo. I draw the bulbous letters of my initials (DAG) and the reversed initials of Randy G, a friend of mine, (GER) in the shape of a dagger. I'm super talented. To add to this, I bring along detailed maps of the whole neighbourhood on a clipboard. I am pretty sure it's only a matter of time before Dean makes me his lieutenant.

Chapter 31: An Episode of Ape

While Mom is at school, Ape and I are latchkey kids, wearing our house key around our necks with a string. Last to leave, I lock up the house each morning. At noon hour, walking the two blocks from St. Thomas, I arrive to my lunch ready for me in a Tupperware container in the fridge. Ape's lunch is there too, but he rarely returns home for the prepared meal due to his varied palate, preferring instead to sample a little of all of the lunches of the stay-at-school kids.

After school, I must return promptly to feed my turtle, then check the mailbox for more documents and photos sent directly to me from Houston or Cape Kennedy. As a self-appointed consultant to NASA, I have kept up with the twelve missions of the Gemini Project and now must always be up-to-date as we start our work on the crucial Apollo moon missions.

Some days after school, whenever Ape has arrived home and is having an "episode," I quickly leave my vital NASA papers and run down the stairs to hide in the tiny narrow closet by the back door. This is where we keep our broom, cleaning supplies, and our General Electric vacuum cleaner.

In the dark, stuffy closet, I sit on the hard metal vacuum cleaner and imagine I am a solo astronaut on one of the old Mercury missions. I feel good as General Electric is one of the companies that help build the rockets.

I often lose track of time in there, suddenly hearing Mom's voice calling me. I open the tiny closet door, see her taking off her coat and putting down her school books, asking where Ape is and why are all the sharp knives on the kitchen table.

Chapter 32: Mental Dental

My school classroom is a constant trauma zone of ear-pulling, head-knocking, hand-strapping discipline. I am a mere passive spectator surrounded and entertained by the suffering of my classmates. As a good boy, I can easily avoid being involved, but I cannot hide from three painful and unavoidable screaming horrors that happen outside of the classroom: a visit to the orthopaedic shoe shop, a visit to the barber, and a visit to our sadistic dentist.

I have flat feet — no arch at all, the full soles of each foot from toe to heel fully touching the ground, my sister making duck quack sounds at the shape of my wet footprints.

Throughout my childhood, I am forced to wear high-arched stiff black orthopaedic Oxford shoes, supposedly to give me an arch. Even my runners have painfully-high arch-supports, which make me run funny. This is the only reason I never receive any ParticipACTION award patches, not even bronze.

Every July and August I am continuously shoeless: running around barefoot, my soles becoming hard as leather, no foot problems in any way. Then September arrives, and the dreaded trip to my arch-villain (Yvette's term.) It is not until the 1970s when forcing flat-footed children to wear corrective shoes is considered a useless, for-profit scam.

A visit to the barber should not be traumatic, but when your mom is on welfare and needs to save money, she sends you to a barber school — literally a school for people learning to be barbers with low-income people as their living mannequins.

At age five or six, there is no dread of an unstylish haircut: only the fear of bleeding ears and bloody gouges everywhere on your head.

"Stay still, kid!" the teacher supervising the student barber would yell as I lose another chunk of skin.

Our "welfare" dentist, Dr. M, is a cruel man without empathy, pulling teeth and filling cavities as fast as he can. Mom often forces us to see him as my sister dubs our family's teeth as "perfectly straight, perfectly rotten." Behind our chicklet smiles are pounds of fillings. We have more lead in our mouths than enamel, with me having the worst of it.

I miss a day of school to be sent by bus by myself downtown to the Mental Dental Building on Rose and 11th. I delay my entrance into hell, looking up seven storeys from the sidewalk to admire this beautiful stone and brick skyscraper, with its cool long-neck gargoyle eavestroughs peering over the top floor.

My next, and last treat before I am filled with pain, is the elevator ride with the little man cheerfully opening and closing the metal scissor-gate and yelling out each floor number. I want to tell him that I promise to give all of my toys to the starving children in China if only I can spend the day going up and down in the elevator with him.

I am pushed out with the rush of parents and screaming children, all being dragged to their own evil doctor or dentist.

"Don't you brush your teeth, kid? You got terrible teeth. Which one hurts?" Dr. M is in my face, his furry ungloved hands wrenching open my mouth, my jawbone nearly getting unhinged.

"I see three fillings, one pull." He leans to the side to pick up a huge metal and glass needle, and shoves it down my throat. I jump as it pierces and penetrates. I feel liquid dripping down my windpipe and I try to cough, struggling to move but he has my arms pinned. Tears are flowing. I'm gagging. "Oh c'mon, boy, you got diapers in those pants?!"

My eyes roll back in my head and my mind thankfully shuts out the shrill drills, sharp scraping, endless ache and pain and drool.

In a haze, I hear a woman's voice from faraway, "You want to keep your tooth?"

I slowly open my eyes and am so happy to find myself on the sidewalk out front again. My whole head is throbbing and when I put my hands on my puffy face I realize I won't be able to fit through the bus doors. I start to walk the thirty blocks home, squeezing the bloody tooth in my hand.

Chapter 33: Shut Up, This is Important

The dual narratives of my 1960s childhood are Jesus and rockets.

I love my Catechism classes: all of the drama of the Bible stories, the pageantry of Mass, the fascinating history of The One True Church. All based on the far distant past. Alongside, as powerful and intriguing, is my deep involvement with NASA and our future space missions.

I cannot recall my first moment of interest in either Catholicism or the space program. I gain permanent membership in The Church as an unknowing newborn, and it seems I have always been part of NASA as well.

No one else in my family has ever had any interest in rockets, so it is a mystery how I stumble upon this obsession that will consume my childhood. As a family, we would always watch the CKCK-TV TelePulse 6 o'clock newscast, so I am guessing I heard anchor Jim McLeod introduce news stories on the first Mercury missions and that is how I got hooked.

In a tiny paragraph I find in a letter that Louis wrote to our mother, he mentions how fascinating and scary the launch of Sputnik in 1957 was to him at age seven. I do not recall him ever mentioning this to me. (Then again, I don't really remember talking to either of my brothers about anything, ever.)

The bedroom I share with Ape is filled with my model rockets, from tiny Mercury ones to the bigger Gemini with fold-out doors, and all the way up to a full Saturn V rocket. All of my paperboy earnings, as well as my Mom's generous monthly allowance and Alfred's random twenty-dollar cheques, go toward the costs of maintaining my professional standing in the NASA space program.

Every evening I go through our local daily newspaper and cut out every space story, my rubber-tip Elmer's glue bottle ready to paste each article into my ever-growing compilation of Hilroy notebooks documenting our race to the moon. It is frustrating whenever a front-page story continues on its own flip-side on page two, making it difficult to scissor-cut a two-sided story without severing any part yet leaving extraneous crap on the edges, such as those Steen & Wright fur ads. At times like these, I am forced to ask my non-NASA mother for help and she does her best.

I also include the rare stories from the Soviet space program. One is a lengthly compilation of all their achievements of the past few years. Needing Mom to help me arrange this lengthly cut-up article into my notebook, I show her a picture of Valentina Tereshkova, the first woman in space in 1963, and I ask why women here do not get to be astronauts. Mom just shrugs. (It takes twenty years nearly to the day before an American woman is in space.)

This really confuses me. As my mom and sister do everything, I naturally assume all women everywhere can do anything they want. Hearing the 'women's lib' stories in the late 1960s is bewildering; I am dumbfounded why there is so much turmoil. Why would anyone care if an astronaut or engineer or doctor was a man or woman? I'm a congenital feminist and didn't even know it.

I am fanatical about only having replicas of real spacecraft and real NASA equipment, no science fiction crap. I dream of buying the full astronaut spacesuit complete with helmet that I see at the back of my comic books, and am shocked when I hear a friend has ordered one and it just arrived. I run over to his place to see him crying in his living-room, packaging around his feet, standing there in a pyjama onesie —complete with feet and a hood— all patterned in a full Mercury astronaut spacesuit. I am on the shag carpet laughing my head off, a total non-supportive friend.

Checking the mailbox the moment I get home each day throughout the school year, I keep up with NASA news with my many subscriptions of mission highlights, glossy photographs of astronauts, and future plans.

After the last day of Grade 3 in late-June 1969, I have no school schedule or obligations and am in a constant tizzy, hardly able to contain the tension leading up to the launch of Apollo Eleven and the first manned moon landing in July. Wearing my winter boots and gloves, I practice exiting the Lunar Module on the moon by climbing down the wooden ladder from the top bunk-bed to the bedroom floor over and over. (I'm sure every kid in the world is doing this.) I know NASA has a full crew, as well as a backup crew, but I still need to be ready in case I am called in at the last minute.

July 20th finally arrives and all morning I am sitting inches in front of our television set, Mom telling me to back up so she can see. (This is the only Sunday I recall not going to Mass.) In early afternoon, as a fuzzy grey blur on our black and white television set, we see Neil start to descend the ladder. Halfway down, there is hysterical screaming outside on our front lawn. Mom runs out of the house to yell at Ape: "Shut up, this is important!" and runs back to sit beside me to hear Neil say, "That's one small step for [a*] man. One giant leap for mankind."

(* It makes me so upset years later when I hear people say Neil screwed up his big line by forgetting the 'a' before man, without which the whole statement makes no sense. I'm on the side that a sudden bit of static hid his 'a' from us.)

Chapter 34: Hippy Headline Hell

I am surprised on how much time I spend with my big sister as we grow up. Here she is, a rebellious teen in the 1960s, always happy and willing to have her dopey little brother hanging around her and her friends. I think she just likes having a little hippy she can dress up.

We all radically change in appearance from 1967 to 1969: from short hair, collared shirts, regular pants—to long hair, wild-coloured shirts, flair jeans. Yvette and Louis are the quintessential hippies, at the perfect age, at the peak of Flower Power. They are floating on top of one of the biggest demographic bulges in our country's history. Their generation's sheer numbers demand attention. It is 1969 — Louis is 19, Yvette 18 ... and I'm nine.

My Grade Four class photo has me with a bright purple shirt, purple leather vest with long jangles, and me with the longest hair for a boy in the class.

I did go to school that morning wearing my purple leather headband and a wooden peace-sign badge that Yvette pinned on me, but a nun points at me and orders me to remove both for the official photo. I am shocked and very upset and I almost say something.

My sister trades in her traditional early-60s "cat's eye" glasses for tinted, round granny glasses. She loves it when I tell her she looks just like Janis Joplin. (I only like looking at one of Joplin's album covers: the one where you can see the outline of an actual nipple.)

Little David is amongst many of Yvette and Louis' fellow hippies, just hanging out in our living room or on the big front lawn of the housing project. There is always music playing on our record player, many boxes of albums beside it. Yvette supplies me with Cokes as I sit in the corner, listening to all the subversive conversations.

Her girlfriends always talk to me, once putting me on the spot in front of everyone when they ask what record they should put on next. I'm blank: I can see Janis's boob right now but can't think of her name, especially with everyone looking at me. I search for a name and out pops:

"Bob Dylan...?" Squeals of joy from the girls, groans from the guys.

Sitting in the corner I also page through lots of colourful, psychedelic magazines — ones with druggie stuff, ones with goofy cartoons, ones with political stuff like Richard Nixon's face cleverly crossed out. I love flipping to the back and seeing all the weird posters you can buy, all with bulbous letters:

Flower Power

Peace Love Music

Keep on the Grass

Turn On Tune In Drop Out

This fun comes to an abrupt end when I see the most offensive thing in my life. I am in shock, start to tremble uncontrollably, burst into tears, and run from the living room — away from these awful people, the terrible music, and those sick magazines.

Chasing me out the door, Yvette finally catches up to me to see what's wrong. I can barely talk.

Telling me to calm down and breathe like Mom taught me, I stutter my incomprehension at what I saw: a poster of the famous front page newspaper story of the first moon landing of Apollo Eleven this past summer.

"What's wrong with that?" she asks.

I get a hold of myself to angrily explain that, instead of a big bold real headline of MAN ON MOON, it says ... WHO CARES?

Chapter 35: Space Cadet

After Mom's funeral, I look through the many boxes of what I call Irene's Archives and never find those few mementos, those pieces of paper from my childhood I wish were there.

She always had a letter-size writing pad, with a lined carbon sheet behind each page, which she used to write all her notes to our teachers:
- an excuse on why I could not go skating
- an apology on why Yvette had once again worn her school uniform skirt too high
- an explanation on why Louis could not financially afford to attend an out-of-town chess tournament
- an acknowledgement of what Ape did and a promise to make him see a doctor.

The papers I would love to have now are the permission slips Mom wrote for me so I could miss school to watch the Apollo moon landings and any part of the ten-day missions from launch to splashdown that I wanted. She was always very supportive of my career.

I don't know why, but the one I most would like to have is the absentee note she wrote on the Monday morning after I watched Apollo 14 land on the moon at 2:18am on 05 February 1971.

> David missed school on Friday as he was awake all
> night watching the moon landing.

The biggest challenge in my NASA position during all of the

Apollo missions—the same is true of everyone at Mission Control in Houston—arrives suddenly with the Apollo 13 explosion in April 1970.

For the first two days, only bits of news are trickling to the public, me being stranded up here in Canada. Speculating what is happening out in space, the TV commentators are interviewing experts who are using hand-held plastic rocket models to demonstrate. To save every ounce of electrical power, there is no live footage being beamed from the disabled spacecraft.

While watching the TV news, I am trying to tune my transistor radio into one of the faraway frequencies I sometimes receive. Perhaps I can get the inside scoop directly from Commander Lovell aboard Odyssey.

Early on the Thursday morning, two days into the crisis, Mom receives a phone call for me to help. My teacher wants me to bring in my large model of the Apollo rocket for Show and Tell. She asks me and of course I say yes, dammit! there are people depending on me.

I do not take my full Saturn V rocket as it is taller than me and can only be carried by two people in a specialized long box that could double as my coffin. I would be a bit nervous doing that, as it has only ever left my home for Science Fairs and that was by car. Instead I only take a separate, oversized model of the Command, Service, and Lunar Modules.

I carefully bundle my spacecraft in its specialized styrofoam jacket, put on my own jacket, then slowly, robotically, walk the short distance to St. Thomas School — the bullies stopped in mid-fist thrust, the losers on their backs on the sidewalk stopped in mid-brace, all looking at me, the science genius.

Once I arrive, I am asked to set up at the front table of the Science Room. This is my big moment. I open one of the bay covers of the Service Module to show the oxygen tanks where NASA is guessing is the cause of the explosion.

My presentation in front of several classes is just a blur to me. All I remember is seeing the face of every boy, even the tough guys, in complete admiration of my technical knowledge. Seeing the face of every girl, dreamingly staring at me, each wishing she will one day be Mrs. David G, wife of a space cadet.

In a moon mission crisis potentially more devastating than the Apollo 13 explosion, I discover—the very evening before the St. Thomas School science fair—that a vital piece of my Saturn V rocket is broken beyond repair.

On my knees on my bedroom floor, staring at this horror, I now know that deep punch-in-the-gut dread that Mission Control felt when they realize the gravity of Apollo 13 astronaut Jack Swigert's words of "Okay, Houston, we've had a problem here."

I don't know how, but the instrument unit of my four-foot-tall Saturn V moon rocket is smashed. This little, vital instrument unit is a ring-shaped structure that sits atop the rocket's third stage. Without which, the whole rocket cannot stand to its full height.

I fly into Mom's room in a sobbing panic, and she brings me back to my room to see what can be done.

I am freaking out, having a complete mental breakdown. "Nothing can be done! It's wrecked! The Science Fair's tomorrow!"

She suggests I present the rocket, not with each stage on top of each other as they would be on the launch pad, but on their sides in various separate pieces for display purposes.

Oh my God, what a bone-headed idea! I'm shaking with frustration at her not knowing that won't be acceptable to my NASA colleagues.

I try to go to sleep that night, tossing and turning thinking about the disaster that awaits me in the morning. I even have nightmares of then-U.S. President Richard Nixon showing up at the Science Fair to yell at me for ruining the space program.

Bleary-eyed the next morning, I stumble downstairs for breakfast and am astounded to find my complete Saturn V moon rocket by the back door, fully standing upright from bottom to top.

My uneducated mother, somehow, with her limited technical knowledge, had fashioned a new instrument unit out of a margarine container — cutting off the bottom, using slivers of the plastic cover for the ridging, and finding my model paint to match the colour of the full rocket.

She grabs me from the depths of Hell and plunks me on top of the Grade 6 Science Fair.

Chapter 36: Ape's Brain

I am thrilled when Ape gets tonsillitis. He will be away in hospital for a few days, a well-deserved peaceful break for Mom, me, and everyone else in our neighbourhood.

In the 1950s and 60s, it is common practice to surgically remove the inflamed tonsils of every child. Though requiring a two or three day hospital stay, it is a simple procedure and is performed in the millions until targeted antibiotics are developed.

As I eagerly watch Mom pack Ape's items to take to the Grey Nuns Hospital, I start to get uneasy as she seems to be packing some of my things too.

She somehow finds me under my bed, lying tight against the wall, my Saturn V rocket case hiding me.

I do not go quietly; I am outraged that I am going to be butchered only because Ape has tonsillitis. With no medical training background at all, Mom tries to explain to me that I am going to have to get my tonsils out one day, so it is best to have the surgery done now. I am horrified and unconvinced until she pulls out her quite persuasive offer: unlimited chicken noodle soup and ice cream after the surgery.

What kid can resist that? I'm in, though slightly haunted by my accidental overhearing of Yvette describing to Ape the possibility that when the doctor cuts his tonsils, the bleeding may not be able to be stopped and Ape may drown on the operating table. I smile at the thought. I ask Mom if that could

140

happen to me too; she has a talk with Yvette.

Mom, as always, comes through with her wonderful promise of unlimited chicken noodle soup and ice cream. If I ever find myself on Death Row, I am definitely going to request these for my last meal.

The only time in my life I am concerned about Ape's health is the short while after we return home from our dual tonsillectomies. Yvette convinces me that whatever happens to Ape, will now happen to me. She has me terrified every time Ape gets a bad cold or is ill for some unknown reason. When he breaks his arm, I brace my arms.

When Ape hits his early teens, he strangely starts to lose weight, his eyes get bulbous, he becomes even more irrational, has more violent episodes. Mom runs out of paintings and pictures to cover the punch-holes in the walls of our house.

After much distress and forced attempts for him to get help, Ape is diagnosed with an overactive thyroid and surgery is the only answer.

My sister comes to her senses and compassionately tells me it has nothing to do with me. The condition comes from Maurice, so I am immune and will not be cut open again. This makes me happy and relieved. She does confide in me that she is quite worried about Ape's surgery, that it is quite serious, that his neck will be cut open ear-to-ear and a large part of his brain will be taken out. I am never to tell that to Ape, and especially never to Mom.

For years afterwards, I am startled every time I'm playing in our root cellar and see the shelves of Mason jars with our preserved fruits and vegetables. Mom is a pack-rat and I wonder if Ape's brain is in a jar somewhere here on the rough wooden shelves, topped with a masking-tape label in her perfect handwriting:

brain, blanched

Chapter 37: Keeping Body Parts

My irrational fear of Mom saving body parts comes true decades later when I am clearing out her house after the funeral.

I rent a seemingly never-ending series of large dumpsters and have them placed on the driveway, while I alone spend an entire summer hauling stuff out of her house and into the dumpsters.

I open a box in her bedroom closet and am freaked out to see teeth, lots and lots of teeth. She has kept every pair of dentures she has ever had. Seeing one's own deceased mother's teeth in a box is a very unnerving sight. I sit on the back step for awhile to get my courage up to remove the box.

Another box, one where Christmas cards are usually kept, is labelled: "Louis 1970." I open it to see it filled with hair — big swatches of bright orange-red hair. I am afraid to look further.

My worst fears are confirmed when I see a large box underneath labelled, "Hair." Though I am hoping it will be filled with her 1970s wigs, it's of course filled with real hair — dozens of plastic baggies full of hair, all clearly labelled in black marker on masking-tape with the name of the donor (voluntarily or secretly), such as:

Yvette, age 1, age 8

Louis, age 4, 6, 7, 10, 13, 18, 20

Sitting alone on the floor in her house, I try to understand yet never discover why she keeps these things. I find objects I understand she keeps for sentimental reasons, but for most, I simply do not understand. I save her photographs, of which she has thousands.

One emotional reunion I have is with Ricky, the human-like doll my mother sews from scratch for a sewing class forty years ago. Ricky is still dressed in my clothes, an exact replica of three-year-old me: same height, same size, same hair and eyes.

I give him one last hug and, for some unknown reason, I stuff all the baggies of hair under his shirt, tuck it tightly into his pants, and place him out at the bottom of the dumpster.

I continue to dig amongst Mom's possessions when I hear odd noises coming from outside. I stick my head out the front door to see what looks to be two people inside the giant dumpster in the driveway.

"Hello! hello!," I say, finally getting their attention. They stand up and smile at me. I don't know what to say.

143

"Um, what are you doing?" They look at each other; one says something to the other in a language I do not understand, then points off to the side of the driveway, to the neighbour's lawn. There sits a broken lamp stand, a scratched-up end table, a couple of ratty chairs.

I stand there, not knowing what to say or do. What's the proper etiquette in this situation? 'Dear Miss Manners: There are several elderly people inside my dumpster. Do I shoo them away or leave them to sort through the junk?'

I just wave and smile, and go back to my work inside the house, piling up the dumpster-bound items in the living room, leaving those people to do what they are doing out on the driveway. I am preserving all of my mother's personal papers and photographs in a designated room in the house, so they can take anything that's out there; whatever they don't remove from the dumpster will be soon buried at the Regina Dump.

At the end of the day, seeing no one in the dumpster, I continue to fill it with many more items from my family's past. As I throw in more and more, I am looking to see exactly what those people thought was of value.

Old kitchen tables, chairs, shelves are gone; mostly broken and stained, but, I suppose, fixable. Surprisingly, they have taken our big, wooden stereo speakers from the 1970s. Gone is a still-working VCR, though they leave the box of videotapes Mom recorded during Pope John Paul II's three visits to Canada.

I am stunned to realize what also is missing is Ricky.

Maybe this whole scam was a ruse to kidnap him. I really do

not know why I am so upset — I had thrown him away in a dumpster. Maybe it's because he is part of my childhood, only my childhood; he cannot be given to a another child.

Then the horror hits me: the hair. I block out the thought that a child will soon be playing with Ricky and out pops ...

Chapter 38: A Village, It Takes

Dollard is stalled at village status when my mother, her husband, and their children live there in the 1950s. The population drops by one when Maurice finally leaves for good. It increases by one when I am born in the summer of 1960, then drops by five a month later when my mother moves the family to the big city of Regina. My father never leaves and is a resident for his entire life.

Dollard eventually dwindles to hamlet status, then dissolves to nothing more than a part of the larger R.M. (Rural Municipality). An internet search finds it on a Ghost Towns of Saskatchewan website.

The house on Railway Avenue where my mother spent her early motherhood years is gone. The house had always been a rough, unpainted wooden house, flush against the wooden sidewalk, leaving no room for a front yard.

Soon after her escape from Vancouver in the early 1950s,

this is where she becomes the Post Mistress of Dollard, running the Post Office out of the main floor of this house. Everyone in the village and surrounding farms enters through a door by the sidewalk, the dust from The Great Sand Hills, thirty miles to the north, rushing in with them.

Sick of all the dust and dirt and sand, this north door was removed, the hole boarded up, and a new door was cut out on the east side of the house – somewhat protected from the constant southeasterly winds.

The idea of a ghost town conjures up images of creaky old wooden buildings, mysterious alleyways, rows of abandoned storefronts. Dollard is a ghost town without any ghosts: almost all of the houses and buildings are gone. Empty is the only word to describe it. The natural prairie will soon consume everything.

Mom and I are standing on the crumbling sidewalk in front of where her house used to be. It is April 2003, over four decades after moving away, and she is looking down at a patch of dry weeds and bits of concrete. We had heard somewhere that the house had been moved intact in the late 1970s to be used as a chicken coop on a nearby farm.

To our right, the huge Dollard Hotel once stood. It too is gone, replaced by weeds. To our left is the only building, the boarded-up Community Centre, standing alone.

Further to our left, the Elementary School where my oldest brother and sister first attended school, is nothing but a large empty lot with a few small, broken trees. We heard the school had been disassembled brick by brick and dispersed elsewhere.

To our right and across Railway Avenue, the two remaining, empty grain elevators stand as silent sentinels to a thriving community that once was.

On our way out of town, we stop by the abandoned Catholic church and cemetery as is the custom. We stare at the white wooden church of Sainte-Jeanne d'Arc (Joan of Arc), its paint peeling, its rotting window frames boarded up, the whole structure on the verge of collapse — its thin wooden steeple still rising high above the flat prairie landscape.

The cemetery is a strange sight, mostly because of its immense size. It is a huge, near-empty field surrounded by a wire fence and a metal gate. The graves, placed along the fence on all four sides, take up only a minuscule portion of the available space. The settlers were thinking big when they designed this cemetery, betting on Dollard becoming a thriving town with a huge population.

In the exact centre of the square cemetery—faraway from the outermost graves along the fence on all four sides—is a tall wooden cross, the graves of two priests, and a cairn noting the name of every priest who had served in the parish from its inception until its closure. I look for the name of who had baptised me in the church now standing abandoned behind us. My mother points to the name and tells me the priest was related to her runaway husband.

Beside the cairn is a curiosity: a large, white wooden box on a stand, its glass front covered in prairie dust. I put my nose to the weathered glass, cup my hands around my eyes to block out the bright sunshine, squinting and struggling to see what is inside this dusty box. I finally focus on a set of creepy eyes, and nearly jump out of my skin.

A three-foot-tall doll of Joan of Arc, dressed in her battle gear, stares at me as I stumble backwards and hit the dry stubble with a thud. Mom just shakes her head.

As we leave Dollard and I am about to turn onto bumpy, broken Highway 13 to go back to Ponteix, Mom has an idea: let's turn the other way and drive twenty kilometres to find our old house.

I find this an absurd quest as we have no details on where exactly it was moved to — all we know is the house is possibly being used as a chicken coop, possibly somewhere near the neighbouring town of Eastend.

As we weave along the potholed highway, I tell her to not get her hopes up. I think the chances of finding it are near zero.

"There it is! Stop, stop, STOP!!!" she yells, making me almost lose control. I pull over onto the gravelly shoulder.

"Bring the camera." She is out of the car before I can say anything.

As the dust settles, I look out to see my mother at a sturdy wooden fence and beyond, in the middle of a large field, a dark-brown wooden structure. I wonder how I can politely tell her this generic structure looks like every other wooden building we have seen today.

"See the door, look at the door," she says, pointing at the

faraway building. I do not see anything but a weathered structure in a farmer's field. "Can't you see the cut-out on the left side?"

I get out of the car for a closer look and there is indeed what looks like a boarded-up front door of a house. I move a little bit along the fence until I see the side of the house and, yes, there is a new door.

"Wow, that's our house," is the only thing I have to say. She is ecstatic she found it.

Chapter 39: The unFrench Revolution

Tracking one's genealogical tree a few generations back, or even dozens, is a worthwhile and important life task to complete but, in the end, may turn out to be quite unsatisfying. Looking at the full chart, all you see a multitude of names and dates and places of birth, of marriage, of death. That's it.

My ten-generation genealogical tree looks the same as one used for genetic experiments in mice (without, I am guessing, the marriage dates.) Family Trees are just impersonal data charts. The crucial parts are missing: the stories. Why did she marry that person? Why did he leave that country? What exactly did his first few wives die of?

Pierre de-Cyr, my first recorded ancestor on my mother's side, leaves France in 1666, age eighteen, and lands here in

New France (Québec.) I will never know why that young man chose to leave his hometown of Orléans, France, to cross the Atlantic by himself.

I know historians hate "what ifs" and alternative histories, but I cannot help wondering ... what if Pierre never leaves France to come over here?

Before he decides to leave Orléans, what if a beautiful girl —let's call her Camille—finally smiles at Pierre as he repeatedly passes by her shop? What if she does smile, does he have the courage to stop and chat with this stunning brunette with the fresh baguettes?

If Pierre and Camille do kiss and fall in love, my genetic destiny will be forever changed.

I am suddenly no longer a Canadian typing his memoirs in forty-below frozen Saskatchewan — I am now lounging in a Parisian café sipping a pert Beaujolais, nibbling on foie gras, enacting Molière with French lingerie models.

"Oh, Dah-veed, tu es si intelligent," says one.

"Et sexy..." the others murmur.

Damn that mythical Camille for ignoring Pierre, and damn that real Pierre for leaving hot France for cold Canada.

But he may not have had a choice. Between 1664 and 1671, about a thousand engagés arrive in New France. These young men are indentured servants, debt slaves, on three-year contracts of hard work to pay back theirs or their family's debt back in France. Afterwards, they are free to return home or to stay. When Pierre arrives, a quarter of the men over the age of fifteen in New France are engagés. I want to know if that is the reason he's here, but I have found no document.

Soon after he arrives, Pierre is listed in the very first census of New France (Québec) in 1666. He is a resident of the settlement of Bécancour, which is on the south shore of the mighty Saint-Lawrence River exactly halfway between Québec City and Montréal. On the opposite shore is Trois-Rivières, the second oldest settlement in New France (after Québec City itself) founded decades before in 1634.

To keep things simple, we call this first known ancestor of ours Pierre I as he has a son named after himself (Pierre II), then a grandson (Pierre III.) Pierre I becomes a farmer and for six generations, spanning 250 years, my family farms this land near Bécancour, Québec.

We would probably still be farmers there if it was not for what members of my family call The English War. Everyone else calls it The Great War or World War One.

For the first few years of the war starting in 1914, all of Canada's soldiers are volunteers. As news of how horrendous conditions are in the battlefield trenches of Europe drift back to Canada, the number of volunteers starts to dwindle. The percentage of volunteers of French Canadian heritage has always been disproportionately very low as this war is perceived in Québec as a British issue.

Guessing that conscription (a.k.a. mandatory draft) may be upcoming in order to get more soldiers over to fight, my great-grandparents are in fear their war-age boys are about to be forced into battle. After centuries of farming the same land in Québec, they decide it is time to run away to save their family.

Renting a freight train car, they fill it with all their possessions. False backs are built into the wooden wardrobes that are placed into the train car; behind these secret walls will live the conscriptable war-age sons until they see the freedom of the west. Their new world is three thousand kilometres away by rail: the prairies of Western Canada, near the settlement of Ponteix in the southwest part of the young province of Saskatchewan.

There are two ways of looking at this decision to leave Québec: enjoy the adventure of opening up new farmland out west, or be seen as running away as cowards of war. Both seem simultaneously fine to me.

Chapter 40: Virgin Mary Miracle

Nearly every settlement on the Canadian prairies owes its birth to the railway, without which no village or town could exist. Though Ponteix owes its prosperity to the railway, it owes its actual birth to the Mother of God.

In 1906, a French priest named Father Albert-Marie Royer crosses the Atlantic in search of a place to establish a parish dedicated to the Virgin Mary. Before he leaves France, he is

152

given a gift from his friend, an antiquary who happens to have a large oak carving of the Pieta.

A pieta is a wooden sculpture showing the Virgin Mary sitting in intense sorrow, the lifeless body of her crucified son draped on her lap. Most pietas are made of wood, except for that one made by the big show-off Michelangelo who carves his out of marble and makes it extra big.

The story of Father Royer's pieta, originally covered in gold leaf, says it was carved in 1475 and was saved from destruction during the French Revolution by pious peasants hiding it in a haystack.

And to this day is credited with at least one miracle.

Guided by God, Father Royer settles in Saskatchewan on the north side of Notukeu Creek. In 1908, he establishes and names both the parish and hamlet Notre Dame d'Auvergne (Our Lady of Auvergne, France.) Everything is fine for this new hamlet and tiny parish until the surprise announcement in 1914 from the Canadian Pacific Railway of a slight change in their original route plan. The CPR is now going to lay track south — not north — of the creek.

Father Royer simply orders the whole community to pick up and move south of the creek to meet the upcoming railway. This must have been a test from God.

Father Royer names the new location Ponteix, after his former parish in France, and when a new church is built, it retains the previous church's name of Notre Dame d'Auvergne.

Only six years later, this second church is completely destroyed by fire, with miraculously the only item saved from the inferno being the pieta.

It is said that two heroic boys break a basement window and find their way in the fire and smoke to the crypt underneath the bell tower to retrieve the pieta. No one can explain how the large wooden sculpture could have possibly fit through the small basement window; therefore, it's a miracle.

A new, spectacular church is built and, to this day, it has the pieta—called Our Lady of Sorrow—resting on a small table directly behind the altar.

Spectacular does not adequately describe this gigantic awe-inspiring church, the one in which I spend all my childhood Christmas Eve Midnight Masses, every Easter Service, a few weddings, and regular family funerals. It is where Mom, all her siblings, her parents, and all relations celebrate their Baptisms, Communions, Confessions, Confirmations, Weddings, and Funerals.

The church is as huge as a Cathedral; in fact, it was built to be a Cathedral. The seating capacity is over nine hundred; the two steeples stand nearly forty metres high with crosses on top roughly seven metres tall; the curved ceiling is a series of massive arches with no columns for support, one arch proclaiming: Mon Âme Glorifie Le Seigneur (roughly: Lord, glorify my soul.)

But, by some horrid twist of fate, St. Philomena, the huge church in Gravelbourg (a francophone town 100km east) gets the Vatican nod in the early 1930s to become the Cathedral of southwest Saskatchewan and the most holy residence of the

Bishop.

Losing the Cathedral designation to damn Gravelbourg is a bitter let-down for proud Ponteix.

(Note: there is some guilty joy many years later when the Vatican strips St. Philomena of her sainthood and the embarrassed Gravelbourg bishop has to change his Cathedral's name in 1965.)

Chapter 41: Voilà Monsieur Thibaut

Both sides of my family and all of my ancestors since the beginning of time are culturally French and religiously Catholic. This puts me in an awkward position: I can fake my way as a Catholic, but I cannot fake being French.

On my 1960 long-form Registration of a Live Birth, it designates my "racial origin" as French. Yes, both parents were raised culturally and linguistically as French Canadians in Saskatchewan, but French as a racial origin? And I love the definition of racial origin on the Saskatchewan government form: "English, Irish, Scottish, French, German, Russian, Ukrainian, etc." Here's a shout-out to all my etc friends.

Everything about my background is French yet I grow up as a complete anglophone, knowing nothing about France and very little about Québec. My known bloodline lives in French Québec for a quarter of a millennium before moving out west to settle in pockets of French communities throughout the prairies.

There is a term for us: pure laine, which literally means pure wool. It refers to the people having the exclusive original ancestry of the French-Canadians with a lineage that is 100% derived from settlers in New France, 1534 to 1763. Whether or not it is an obsolete term depends on who you ask; and whether or not it is a racist term depends on who you ask. I find terms like pure laine to be biologically, scientifically, and culturally ludicrous. French as a race is laughable.

I am the reason Québec separatists are fighting to preserve their enclave of French language, customs, and culture in the gigantic sea of English on this continent. Here I am, a product of many generations of pure laine stock, all erased in one childhood. And in a final unknowing act of demolition when I am twenty-two, I make the decision to change all my names to Anglo ones, thereby making the cultural transition complete.

At the family farmhouse, where our mother grows up and where we spend our Christmases and Easters, French is spoken as much as English, though us kids, all my first-cousins and siblings, with me as the youngest, only learn to speak English.

Hiding around the corner, I listen in on my aunts and grandparents and my mom to catch what they are saying about me but it's pointless: when my name is mentioned, and it rarely is, all I hear in French is "Blah blah blah, Dah-veed, blah-blah-blah lune, blah-blah-blah ..."

My sister has a hilarious routine of sounding like she is fluently French to non-French speakers, while babbling nonsense. When asked if she speaks any French, she answers with something like:

"Oui, oui, un petit," using a loud and fake accent, with wild hand gestures.

"Errrr garcon, au contraire croissant, er, cul-de-sac attaché, err, err, how do you say in Hinglish? ... renaissance lingerie vis-à-vis, n'est-ce pas?"

Unilingual English speakers fall in love with her sensual French accent; French speakers wonder if she's having a stroke.

"Crème brulée escargot, errrr, femme fatale derriere, heh-heh-heh! Ménage à trois, vive la différence!"

With her cultural background, Mom, as a new elementary school teacher, is heavily pressured to teach the mandatory French classes to Grade sevens and eights. This is something she does not want to do. She specializes in early childhood education and loves teaching the early grades, so full of promise and curiosity. She is dreading the effort she will need to teach the older kids something that most do not want to learn, the many hours in a silent classroom continually trying to pry some sort of answer out of these kids with their arms crossed or heads on their desks.

I am never that rude to the French teacher in my school. I productively use French class to perfect my flip-book drawings of the moon missions.

I can only assume how disappointed my teacher is when she

meets me—the son of another French teacher, one with a true cultural lineage—to realize I know nothing. Her summer dream of me leading the other students in the learning of this romantic language for the upcoming year is quickly crushed on that first day.

As a consolation, knowing I am on the high-tech super-cool A.V. team, she does put my technical prowess into good use by delegating me to set up the slide-strip projector and French tapes for each dreaded lesson of Voix et Images de France. I am also the one she appoints to hold the big cord, listening for the beep, and pushing the button to advance the frame.

I am the technical producer for Monsieur et Madame Thibaut's show but have no idea what they are saying to my sleepy classmates.

Chapter 42: The G Hug

My sister calls it "The G Hug" — our family's exclusive hug. Like any tai chi position or yoga pose, it looks difficult at first but becomes easy with practice.

Push both shoulders forward, arch your upper back, outstretch both arms on either side of the other person — being careful not to touch — bend elbows, turn hands inwards, then lightly and briefly touch the person's back with your fingertips. Immediately return to upright position. During the process, do

158

not say anything or make any type of noise or do anything with your lips.

It's 1973, Mom and Yvette are standing on the platform at the Regina Train Station, waiting for the middle-of-the-night arrival of the Trans-Canada passenger train. My sister has graduated from Nursing School at the Regina General Hospital and is on her way to Montréal for her first career job. The train arrives, Yvette picks up her bags, stands up and is frozen when Mom gives her first full, warm, close, touching hug — verging on an embrace.

My sister later says she was so startled she never slept for the whole two-day trip, knowing she was going to soon die, her mother having given her the hug of death.

I am guessing Mom inherits this style of hug from her parents, not that I can recall seeing them make an attempt at a hug to anyone, ever.

Not a huggy family is an understatement.

The exception is Yvette and I. She hugs me a lot. I think she considers me her little rag-doll.

It goes without saying that my brother Ape and I never hug. The only physical contact I have with him is his fists.

"Don't hit him in the back!" Mom yells at him every time she pulls him off beating me. She does not want the extra burden of a disabled child.

I start to hug Mom only during return visits to Regina after moving away in my late-twenties. These hugs are rationed to arrival and departure only. Except once.

Several years before her death, she has a growth surgically removed from a space between her skull and brain. I fly back to Regina to help her during her surgery and recovery as Ape, who lives close-by, is "not good with these kind of things."

Mom is calm as I shave her head at her home and bring her to the hospital. She is attentive and receptive to all medical instructions given. I am quite impressed; I thought this was going to be a battle. When the porter arrives, she suddenly asks for a hug from me. I am bewildered and flustered — I've never been asked to do something like this before. I lean over and we embrace, though the memory of her giving my sister the hug of death on the train platform does pop in my mind.

Holding hands, walking beside her as the porter pushes her stretcher down the hallways, we arrive at the Operating Area doors and have to part hands. As she is wheeled away, she looks back at me and says another one of her ill-timed dagger-in-the-heart quips: "I always knew you'd be the one to take care of me."

I make the mistake of marrying into a very huggy family, one verging on pathological. Every hello and good-bye, every accomplishment and milestone, damn near everything is celebrated with hugs and kisses and the archaic "Love you."

Though we both did, Mom and I never once say that out loud to each other.

Chapter 43: I Wish You a Merry Christmas

Every happy Christmas of the 1960s starts with Mom's sister and brother-in-law, Eva and George, arriving at our house in their giant station wagon packed with their three kids, a dog, and all their luggage and Christmas gifts. They live in Moosomin, two hours east on the TransCanada Highway near the Manitoba border. Once in Regina, they stop to cram in my Mom, us four kids, and our luggage and gifts. Off to Ponteix we go in forty-below: ten people and a dog.

As the youngest, cousin Dianne and I are placed in the very back of the station wagon, perfect for us to make faces out the back window at the terrified drivers we pass in a blur. Uncle George will always be my life's fastest and most exciting driver, passing any car, any time, any weather, blind curve or not, Auntie Eva screaming, "GEORGE! Oncoming! Move over!!!"

Ape is not allowed in the back as he likes to roll down the rear window and throw things out onto the highway.

The one and only moving film of my entire family is taken on Christmas Day 1970. The footage is shot by my Aunt E with her Super 8 film camera and its blinding camera light. Forty years later, the film footage is transferred to DVD video and becomes my most cherished possession as it shows the bond my sister and I have.

Us five members of the G Family are sitting in a row on the carpet in front of the Christmas tree showing Ape, age 14; Mom, 39; Yvette, 19; me, 10; Louis, 20. The camera pans from

161

left to right, first showing Ape in his blue silk shirt, purple pants, wide white belt. Mom is next in a sharp-looking salmon pantsuit with a poofy white shirt. Yvette, her long straight jet-black hair tied back in a ponytail, round granny glasses, and barely wearing a blue white-dotted one-piece mini skirt/top. Snuggled up to Yvette is me: gold shirt, brown velour pants, overgrown mop-top. Behind me, always trying to disappear, is Louis: long, fuzzy red hair, dark-rimmed glasses, dark blue shirt, looking away from the camera, smoking a cigarette, the top of his Export A package visible in his shirt pocket.

The part of the video I cherish so much is the brief interaction between my sister and I. As the camera pans from left to right—from Ape to Mom to Yvette to me to Louis—my sister leans close to me, whispers something, makes a peace sign with her left hand, encouraging me to do the same. I always do everything she asks me to do — I'm Yvette's little hippy. I flip a big peace sign directly to the camera. Mom and Yvette have huge smiles.

I have lots of photos of my sister and I, but this 1970 Christmas choppy film clip, to me, shows the close bond we always have for each other until she disappears in 1989.

Chapter 44: Last Family on Earth

My Grandma has the first artificial Christmas tree I ever see,

162

its silver tinsel pine needles slowly changing colour from red to green to blue to yellow as the revolving light machine on the floor spins its disc. Yvette is constantly making snide comments. I'm not sure why she is so antagonistic towards this frail metal tree.

It is set up in the long living room of Grandma and Grandpa's in-town house. This is the Christmas holiday destination for our family and the families of all of Mom's siblings (except Anna, the oldest, the model in New York City, who never returns.)

Throughout the 1960s, it's a full house at Christmastime in Ponteix: Mom and us four kids; her sister Eva, husband, their three kids; her sister Alice and husband (two kids to arrive later); her little brother Raymond and his new wife (two kids to arrive later as well); plus Aunt Thérèse. Seventeen of us in the 1960s, growing to twenty-one in the 70s.

I love hanging out with all my cousins and uncles and aunts for a few days. There are many meals and seemingly no end to the dessert dainties. I don't mind that Grandma never talks to me: she doesn't interact with any of her grandchildren. Though Yvette says that Grandma hates me because I am a bastard, I'm treated exactly the same as all my cousins: all of us equally ignored. (Grandpa, stone-deaf, acknowledges his grandchildren by nodding a lot.)

The only downside of staying at Grandma's house is the nighttime sharing a bed with Ape. I beg Mom to allow me to sleep with her, but that is not possible: Grandma's rule is all adults upstairs, all children downstairs. It hurts when Yvette and the older cousins tease and laugh at me when I try to negotiate sleeping with Dianne, the cousin my age. I don't understand why a boy and a girl can't sleep together; when I have nightmares at home, I often crawl into bed with Mom or my sister.

All of the bed mattresses in the basement are old and saggy. Being in one with Ape terrifies me. I try to think happy thoughts lying there on the edge, wearing my new soft flannel pyjamas, my nose snuggled into my elbow, smelling the newness. It is hard to fall asleep when you are concentrating on staying stiff straight on the high edge, in fear of sliding down the drooping slope to the valley.

I wake up screaming in the dark, Ape punching me hard in my back, yelling "Stop being a ball! Stop being a ball!" From around the room I hear "Shut up you two and go to sleep!"

I wiggle up to my edge of the bed and wait, my back throbbing, crying that no one came to my rescue. I am never going to sleep ever again. That'll teach them.

Again I wake up screaming, Ape punching me in the back, yelling "Stop being a ball!" Seems I do slide down towards the centre of the saggy mattress as I fall asleep in the fetal position: my knees tight against my belly, my head bowed down, my arms wrapped around my head, my bum pushing outwards, touching Ape in his sleep.

We are the last family on Earth to open our Christmas presents, even taking into consideration the global time-zones. We do not open ours on Christmas Eve, we do not open ours on Christmas morning, nor even anytime that whole afternoon. Only after the whole of Christendom is enjoying the material benefits of the season are us kids allowed to open our gifts on the evening of December 25 — but only after dinner, after dessert, and even after Uncle H, the slowest eater in the world, has finished.

You would think the adults would have been driven mad by the constant asking and whining of us kids throughout dinner. Grandma's solution is quite simple: every non-adult eats dinner faraway in a separate food prep room, not in the main dining room/kitchen area. All of us kids sat at a big work table where our food would be plopped down in pots and dishes, the door closed.

Full disclosure: us kids are allowed to open one and only one gift after breakfast on Christmas Day.

We spend many hours examining, holding, measuring, weighing, tilting everything under the silver tree with our name on it. We have only one choice and one chance. By noon, all of my older siblings and cousins have designated their first gift and so have I. We present our one present to a parent for final approval, then run crazy to a corner to open it.

We almost always nail it: with all the time and effort figuring out the hidden gift, we are quite satisfied for the entire day. That is, until I convince myself the small, flat rectangular box has my new super magnifying glass, the one I will use to identify any alien pollen that appears to be on every surface. Squeals of delight from everyone upon opening their prime present, except me. I don't know how I miscalculated so badly.

Starting the moment the Simpsons-Sears Christmas Wish Book is dropped off in our mailbox at home every September, every kid in Canada examines every page of this extravaganza of fun.

The Wish Book is a separate kids' toy catalogue from the regular thick Simpsons-Sears catalogue, the one with photos of bare naked ladies with bras on pages 80 to 91. I once nearly died when I saw a sales flyer with the slogan: 'Bras Half Off!'

Dog-eared after being flip-folded hundreds of times over several months of intense study, the Wish Book is exactly what those kind people at Simpsons-Sears thought was going to become of their catalogue creation. Mom asks us to make a list of the ten toys in the Wish Book that we would love to have. With her poverty income, she promises each one of us will receive one item from our list of ten.

Weeks are spent narrowing down the choices. I still do not know how she does it, but every Christmas without fail we do receive at least one, sometimes more, chosen toy from our Top Ten list from the Wish Book catalogue.

Back to Christmas morning and our task is to choose one gift to play with for the rest of the day — until we can open our many other gifts that evening after dinner, after dessert, the last family on Earth.

Being of superior intelligence, I quickly deduce my thin, rectangular present is the super magnifying glass that is on the

Top Ten list I registered with my mother.

"Shit shit sheeeeeeeee-it!" is Ape's happy, thrilled response to seeing his morning gift: a green plastic army tank with orange bullets that shoot out at great speed. Running out in the snow, shooting at his enemies, he quickly loses all the bullets and throws the "piece of shit" tank at the garage.

My older siblings and cousins are supremely impressed with their gifts of clothes and perfume or cologne, probably Hai Karate. I don't recall anyone receiving a book. For great dramatic effect, I wait until everyone has revealed their gift before opening my package to a devastating result.

It is not my magnifying glass — it's a wallet. I have a leather wallet to play with all day.

I walk up and down the back alley that day, all alone, flipping open my new wallet, flipping it closed, over and over. The neighbours along the street know my grandparents have one grandchild who is "special." Seeing my behaviour that day confirms it must be that weird kid out back in the snow playing with a wallet.

Chapter 45: Awful Christmas Car Problems

One Christmas in the early 1990s, I return home to share Christmas Dinner with Mom. Yvette lives in the long-term care hospital, but Mom has somehow arranged a day pass to bring my sister home from the hospital for the day.

On the stove in a pot is a boiling roast which Mom states is lamb. (It's not: it's mutton; lamb is sweet, tender, and young; mutton is old, tough, and stinky.) Another pot boils potatoes, another has turnip mash.

While this colourless meal boils, Mom reads aloud the medical report of my sister's latest surgery: "The bore hole entered the skull at ..."

I am trying to tune out my mother's voice while suppressing my intense need to search my sister's eyes once again for a spark of recognition, an acknowledgement of where she is. With too many tears over too many years, I stop myself from looking in her eyes and pleading, "Yvette, where are you???"

Mom is on the opposite side of her small square kitchen table from me, head down, monotonously reading the medical notes. My sister is to my right, her head bopping, her left hand squeezing my right hand. I am unable to cry as I am distracted by the guttural sobs of the woman on the fourth side of the table.

She is J, one of my sister's friends from back in Nursing School in the 1970s. She is there to support my mother, to be with her friend, but mostly to be with other people on Christmas Eve. She is recently divorced and does not want to be alone this Christmas as the last two Christmases saw her mother and brother kill themselves.

There is an exact moment in your life where nothing makes sense, where you do not feel what is happening is real, where your world seems to be spinning around you.

Sitting there at Mom's kitchen table on that Christmas Eve is that moment for me: the vile smell of boiling mutton, my beloved blank sister's gasps and spits, my mother robotically reciting horrific surgical procedures, my sister's friend staring at her knife.

Throughout the day, Mom is upset that Ape has not yet arrived back in Regina for Christmas. He is working out on the west coast and promised he would drive back. She knows her favourite child, Louis, will never return to Saskatchewan for Christmas, though he does always call collect on the 24th.

For hours, Mom bugs me to phone Ape, to make sure he has left Vancouver. Before the era of cell phones, a telephone answering message would probably mean he is on his way. I finally break down and say I will call. I don't think I've ever phoned him in my entire life and don't know what the hell I'm going to say.

I am surprised when Ape answers with his guttural hello of "Huuhh."

I say who I am, that I am with Mom, that she is wondering if he is coming home for Christmas.

"Some dumb cunt nicked my truck," he says.

I muffle the receiver, take a long pause, and tell Mom "he's having car problems."

She is upset and tells me to tell him she'll wire him the

money to take the bus, she really needs him here, she'll pay the full Greyhound fare here and back.

"Won't catch me fucken dead on a cock-sucking hound."

I again muffle the receiver, and say "He prefers not taking the bus."

Mom grabs the phone and starts pleading for him to please please come home for Christmas. After several hello? hello? hello? she realizes Ape has hung up. She silently hangs up the receiver, devastated, slowly sits back in her chair. I feel so awful for her; I feel so awful for myself and my lost sister; all of this is so awful.

Chapter 46: Can I have a Heineken?

The first day of June 1989 sees me looking back at my sister, my nose on the glass window of a Greyhound pulling out of the Chilliwack BC bus depot, watching her disappear as she waves goodbye like a lunatic. I am on my way back to Regina, tail between my legs, a total failure. Yvette had begged me to stay, to try again, but I know it's useless.

As many prairie kids do, I had ventured to the west coast to make it big. I had professional television scriptwriting credits, many freelance writing contracts, and a successful one-act play. I was so above the dinky-town of Regina — Vancouver was going to be my limousine ride to the top.

I am booked at New Talent Nights at comedy clubs throughout the Vancouver area. All I need is eight minutes in front of a crowd with a mike. My first club is nearby in Gastown and I am flattered the club is full on a Tuesday evening.

I wait back stage, ignoring the shtick of the buffoons and losers before me. Of course dink jokes get big laughs; I am far more cerebral than that.

I am surprised I don't get even a smattering of applause when my name is announced. Audio system may be faulty. I am perfectly on my mark cue, bright spotlight in my face, silhouettes of people throughout the club, red candles on each little table, clinkling of ice in rye & cokes, my mike in hand.

After my first few hilarious jokes are inconceivably met with dead silence, I'm really concerned there are technical audio problems. I look over to the glass-enclosed audio booth in the corner and the audio guy looks like he is hysterically laughing. I make eye contact and he gives me a big thumbs-up.

I continue my finely tuned set of political and religious observational humour and continue to be met with dead-silent indifference. The whole audience cannot be morons I tell myself. I throw a few more of my brilliant witticisms and it remains a silent, surreal scene: the audio guy laughing his head off in his mime box at every joke, the breathing audience in front of me in the dark. I build up to my big finale and blast out the hilarious final joke.

I hear nothing, absolutely nothing. I look at the boxed-in audio guy and he's banging his table, howling with silent laughter. I look back at the stoic crowd, and get excited when I see an arm rise somewhere in the audience —this is good— a little interaction might let me get off stage gracefully. I eagerly look over to hear "Can I have a Heineken?"

The room instantly fills with loud chatter, chair movement, and I-gotta-pees.

The spotlight shuts off. I'm blind on the dark stage, having trouble getting the microphone back on the stand, squealing feedback. I leave the club, walking alone in the nighttime rain to Downtown Eastside, where I climb the stairs to my flophouse room at the Austin Hotel on Granville Street. Yelling over the blaring music of the main-floor strip club, I phone the other comedy clubs to cancel all of my bookings.

My sister was not at my standup comedy act as I did not tell her about it. I wanted to perform a few shows to iron out whatever wrinkles there possibly could be before having her watch my break-out show.

The next day I take the bus from downtown Vancouver to Chilliwack to tell her of my experience. She begs me to do my full eight minutes for her. Knowing she is my biggest supporter, I do the whole act. She's going to love the big zinger at the end for sure.

It doesn't go well. After the finale, she is quiet, struggling to find encouragement. "David, you must go on stage again. Write more bits, maybe a whole new act — and this time, um, maybe one with jokes."

During my twenty-four hour bus ride from mountains to flatlands, I do write another comedy routine — just for her. I'm laughing by myself in the back of the bus; no one sits near me. Once I arrive home in Regina, I take a few more days to perfect it. When I think it's ready, I get the phone call of her brain explosion.

PART FIVE: DEATH

Chapter 47: My One Parental Kiss

My first memory of seeing my father and mother together in the same room is when I'm 42.

It is in a hospital room a few weeks before his death. It's also the first and only time I see my parents hug and kiss, I the only witness to their final goodbye. Alfred will die of prostate cancer; later, Irene will die of a brain seizure. As I am their sole mutual biological child, I am afraid my death will be caused by either my brain or my bum.

Mom and I enter my father's room in Shaunavon Union Hospital, the hospital where I was born. Alfred raises himself slightly by grabbing on the metal bar of his bed with one thin arm and gives my mom an awkward hug. She sits down in the chair I have pulled up for her, up against his hospital bed, my chair right beside.

They begin talking immediately, oblivious of me sitting there. They look so animated and happy. They talk about many people they both know and who is where and whose kids married who. They seem to talk like they have talked to each other every day of their lives, though they have spent the last forty years three hours apart.

Mom, always the shutterbug, demands photographs. She pulls out her camera and I pose with Alfred on his bed. She and I switch positions and the moment she sits on the bed, his arm around her, his eyes light up with a mischievous glint. As I stand there in the little hospital room, looking into the restrictive camera viewfinder, trying to frame my mother and father sitting on the bed, they are whispering to each other. He has a big smile on his face; she seems to be blushing.

We are there for about an hour, having a great visit, when my mom bolts up from her chair and says "It's time I go." She quickly leans forward and gives Alfred a long hard hug, kisses him, and runs out of the room hiding her face.

The suddenness of her actions surprises me and when I look back at Alfred, his face seems to be in shock, which slowly turns to trembles and tears.

A nurse checks in and Alfred grabs her forearm, clears his throat, and somehow manages: "I want you to meet my son."

She smiles and gives me a big wink with the eye away from him, which I take to mean, "Ignore that – it's the drugs talking." I don't take offence as that was the first time I ever heard him say he was my father.

The first and only time we hug is the last time I see him. I am leaving and we are standing in the doorway of his hospital room — he's struggling to remain standing, gripping his walker. We say our good-byes, then, as I am about to walk away, I turn back to give him an awkward one-arm hug around him and his walker. He is startled by my action — the last image I have is a side-view of him quickly hobbling into his room, tears pouring down his face.

A week later, when I am back home, I receive the phone-call from his lawyer/executor that Alfred has died. I drive back to

Shaunavon with my wife. Mom drives there by herself from Regina, the exact solo trip Alfred did 42 years ago after he dropped her and their newborn child off in the Queen City and returned home alone.

We have no idea who will be at his funeral. I have never met anyone in his family, and I have no idea how big or small it is. Mom is terrified as she has never had any contact with any of Alfred's relatives since she ran away in humiliation over four decades ago, carrying her children and bastard baby.

Us three meekly, tentatively, enter Christ the King Roman Catholic Church and the friendly usher asks, "Family or friends?"

"Um, um, ah —" is all I say.

The usher's face lights up. "You're the boy! Follow me."

We are seated in the front row.

The service is quite simple, with the priest excusing himself to allow a lay person to read the eulogy, which is the newspaper obituary. It ends with:

> … is survived by one son, one sister, one brother, one sister-in-law, numerous nieces and nephews, and his good friend of many years, Irene, the mother of his son.

Mom has her head down, sobbing.

Chapter 48: Funeral Photos

I have been to bad weddings but I have never been to a bad funeral. When I say bad, I mean poorly organized or boring or disastrous or stupid or one that ends in a fistfight down a stairwell. These have happened at weddings I've attended but never at funerals, though I've been at far more funerals than weddings in my life.

I really like attending funerals, not because someone has died—which is sad in over half of cases—but because of how everyone comes together to honour this person's life. To toot my own horn, I must say the best funeral I attend is the dual-funeral I direct for my mother and sister in 2009, complete with a complimentary photo-filled glossy memorial titled, The Story of Two Women. I still get compliments on it.

I see my first dead person when I am ten. It's my Aunt Anna, who dies young of stomach cancer. She is my mother's oldest sister, and the first one to move away from the farm and straight to Montréal where she becomes a model, later moving to New York City in the 1960s to continue her career.

I inherit a beautiful, leather-bound photo portfolio of Anna's work. Yvette always claimed our aunt was in Vogue but I have not yet found any proof of that.

As a New York model, Anna sends her struggling little sister —my mom—her hand-me-down fashions from the previous season, though still many many fashion years ahead of the Canadian prairies.

My mother is the best dressed woman on welfare in Regina in the 1960s.

It gets her in big trouble once at the welfare office when she forgets to dress-down, stupidly showing up in a Chanel suit. It takes all of my mom's energy to convince the petty provincial bureaucrat that our family should not be cut off welfare, that she does not have a rich sugar daddy somewhere. Pleading her case looking like Jackie Kennedy must have been tough, but she pulls through.

When Anna is diagnosed with terminal cancer in New York City, she is flown back to the Canadian prairies and dies in the Regina General Hospital at age 43. Her funeral, back in the family hometown of Ponteix, is my first.

Seeing her in the open coffin does not seem to bother me. It's the sombre family portrait photos of all of us standing in an arc around her that unnerves me. It must be a Catholic thing as we have many family photos taken around every open coffin through the years.

I am so grateful my mother was a prolific photographer of every important event in our family's life, but I cannot accept her need to document death. Many are close-up headshots of the deceased.

Photographs are the most important artefacts in my life and I treasure them above any other physical object, but I do destroy all of the dead relative photos I find in her house after her own death. I rip into shreds the photos of dead Grandma, Grandpa, Aunt Anna, Uncle R, and many other relatives.

A few days after Anna's funeral in Ponteix, we visit my Grandma in the Swift Current hospital. She is very ill and was unable to attend her daughter's funeral. In fact, she doesn't even know about the sad event.

It is in that long, echoey hospital ward, at my Grandma's bedside in a row of beds, where I witness my mother clearly lie for the first time in my life.

Grandma gets the energy to mumble, "Anna?", and my mom answers, "She's fine."

My head bolts up, wide-eyed. My sister nudges me, a finger to her lips. This is damn confusing and a bit scary: I just witnessed my mother calmly and knowingly commit a venial sin, and realize for the first time in my life that my mother is not perfect.

The Ponteix Cemetery is a beautiful place, as are most cemeteries to me. Created in 1914, it has a wide variety of tombstones, headstones, and gravestones. Our family's choice seems to be the flat, horizontal full-grave covering with a small, raised-name headstone.

After each funeral Mass, it is a short walk out the front door of the church and around to the cemetery behind, but we never do that. We always get into our cars out front and drive to it. We enter the cemetery by driving under the metal archway, above us the words:

AU CIEL JIRAI JE VOIR

IN HEAVEN WE WILL MEET

Parking on an empty, dry dirt patch off to the side, we get out of the cars and stroll to the open grave, often stopping to comment on tombstones that catch our attention.

Distracted and not watching where we are stepping, there is always someone who twists their ankle in a gopher hole. Some yell out a painful curse — a blasphemy surprisingly not a sin in Saskatchewan.

There is something I have always noticed and have always been scared to ask anyone about: those few lonely graves on the other side of the metal fence of the Ponteix Cemetery.

I figure they must be suicides, as I have been taught in Catechism that Catholics cannot be buried in consecrated ground if they commit the sin of suicide. Strangely, you can be buried inside the cemetery if you are a murderer and confess your sins to a priest.

Strict Church dogma dictates there are several other conditions where a deceased Catholic cannot be buried in consecrated soil. If you are a notorious sinner who dies without repentance. If you have openly held the sacraments in contempt and show no signs of sorrow. If you are a monk or a nun and are found to have died in the possession of money or valuables which you have kept for your own. If you are killed in a duel. And if you have directed your body to be cremated after death.

It is only when I'm an adult do I finally get the courage to ask someone about those lonely graves outside the cemetery fence, amongst the weeds and abandoned farm machinery.

As we are walking back to our cars after a graveside service, I choose to pose the question to my aunt who I think is the most liberal.

"Oh those?" she casually says, not looking back to where I'm pointing. "Those are just Protestants," she says with a backward flip of her hand.

My first opportunity to be a pallbearer is for my grandpa's funeral, which I take as a great honour. I am only eleven when my Grandma dies, far too young to help carry a coffin, but am twenty-eight at my Grandpa's funeral.

I thought being a pallbearer would be a symbolic, easy task; little did I realize the weight of a coffin.

After my Grandma dies in 1972, all my Grandpa did was wait in his tiny room in the old folks' home, waiting to join her. When he finally dies seventeen years later, his body has shrunk to a wisp.

I happily accept the task of being one of his six pallbearers, not knowing he had picked out one of the heaviest coffins ever built. Myself and the other five larger men must strain to carry it down the church steps and into the hearse.

At the time of his funeral, the main church was undergoing renovations, so all services are being held in the small church hall. The front of the building has a narrow stairway to the sidewalk, made even more narrow with the installation of several metal arm rails. This means we must not only carry the heavy coffin, we must lift it high over these handrails.

I am in the middle on the left side as we descend the steps

we cannot see, the muscles of my right arm bursting in pain, my right hand grasping the handle high at my armpit, my left hand pushing down and inching along the handrail.

Thinking it's only me in trouble, I take a quick glance and am horrified to see the other pallbearers's bright red faces and bulging neck veins. The strain of the weight and the tight squeeze against the handrail is making me quite nauseous; I start to panic as I am about to vomit. I force myself to think happy thoughts, successfully suppressing the horrific gravity of the sin of throwing up on a blessed coffin.

Coffins are beautiful works of craftsmanship and art. It is a pity they are only on public display for a few hours before being buried forever in the prairie dirt.

The many family funerals I attend all feature well-built, solid wood coffins, mostly oak I'm guessing. I feel guilty now: I should have spent more time thinking about the repose of the deceased person's soul during the Requiem Mass rather than admiring the wood finish and copper accessories.

My only shock ever at a funeral Mass is the one for a relative when there is no coffin in sight in the aisle of the Ponteix church. I am terribly confused: there should be no reason the body is not in a coffin in the centre aisle, as usual.

A son recites a brief eulogy, the Mass commences, and continues in its usual process, though when Communion is offered I am stunned with another revelation: less than half of my family—aunts, uncles, cousins—leave their comfortable pews to go up to eat the body of Christ and drink his blood.

I myself have never accepted Communion for over thirty years but I naively assumed everyone else had always stayed on the Catholic path. Seeing so few of my relatives follow my mother to the front is a pivotal religious event in my life.

But the most startling part of the funeral Mass is at the end: the family procession out of the church, fronted by a teary-eyed cousin carrying an urn. This is the first-known cremation burial in my entire family's history; I always thought this was so against Catholic protocol.

Little did most of us know the Roman Catholic Church had reluctantly lifted its prohibition on cremation a decade prior. News travels slow from the Vatican to Saskatchewan.

But what is so absurd at this groundbreaking funeral is the shape of the urn: it is a tiny rectangular coffin, complete with tiny pallbearer handles.

Everyone in the immediate family is crying as they walk down the wide centre aisle. Everyone else giving the grieving family sorrowful nods as the urn passes. Everyone, that is, except me — I am staring, wide-mouth at the urn.

I am so happy Yvette wasn't there: she'd have pissed herself with laughter at this Barbie funeral.

Chapter 49: First-born Funeral

In 2003, the emaciated body of Louis is discovered on the floor of his dark apartment in skid row Vancouver. The apartment manager has my mother's name, address, and phone number and gives all to the Vancouver police, who send the information to the Regina Police, who show up on her doorstep with the sad news.

When she opens the door, one of the officers says, "I'm sorry, ma'am, but we have bad news concerning ... Maurice G —."

"I haven't seen him for fifty years and couldn't care less! Good-bye!" she says, and slams the door in the faces of the police officers.

I only know my mother's version of this story; I can only speculate what went through the minds of these confused officers. They must have looked at each other, one nudging the other to knock again.

When she answers again, she is told, "We have information on the death of, um, Maurice, ah, Louis ... G. Are you his mother?"

Mom and I fly to Vancouver to get the urn and bring it back to the prairies. I had offered to also pay for Ape's flight and hotel but he said he could not take time off: "some people have to work for a living, ya know."

Mom and I get a surprisingly affordable hotel room in Vancouver's Downtown EastSide, a few blocks away from Louis' low-to-no-income housing project on Helmcken Street.

There is no English word to describe what it is like to enter that narrow apartment, locked since his body was removed. Stuffy is the closest word but is still far off. The apartment manager unlocks the door, opens it, and startles us by quickly bending over — flailing to find something to hang on. He pushes back past us and stumbles down the hallway, hacking.

For three days, Louis' huffy oxygen tank kept inflating and deflating his dead lungs. Only after three days of dropping off the government-paid packaged meals delivered inside the door and seeing the previous packages untouched did the deliverer notify the manager.

I repeatedly flip the light switch by the door but nothing turns on. Both Mom and I later describe our steps into the apartment as slow-motion walking underwater. It is dark, with a little bit of light coming in from between what looks like drapes on the far wall. We see vague shapes of things, nothing discernible.

I somehow stumble to the far side — tripping, slipping, kicking who knows what — to open the drapes and to look back at the room: to see Mom paralyzed partway into the hell of her dream child's life.

"What did you EXPECT? He was a JUNKIE all his life in downtown Vancouver!" I yell at her in my head.

She was so proud of him in the late 1990s when she bought him an expensive laptop and he started taking a computer course at a neighbourhood library. His letters describe his excitement of the wondrous world of computers, the emerging internet, his dexterity at the keyboard despite his partially paralyzed right arm. She seems giddy on the phone to me when she describes how he predicts the future of electronic mail.

I bite my lip. At the time, I am working in Ottawa at National Headquarters of Computers Systems for the Federal Government of Canada. When I tell her I am part of the technical team that recently received a prestigious award for a nation-wide computer communications program, she asks if I have a laptop similar to the one she bought for Louis and if I know all the amazing things it can do.

I say I do have quite a high-tech laptop, one I can use to directly log into the four financial mainframes of the Government of Canada using an ever-changing passcode that is sent via satellite to a metal card I carry around at all times. She asks me what kind of printer she should buy Louis.

Her later letters repeatedly ask him how he is doing with his computer courses. After several non-responses, he offers a feeble excuse that someone stole the laptop, then admits he sold it. She tells him she understands, as the price of food in Vancouver has become ridiculous.

Mom had last seen him in this very place a few years ago, but claims it was nothing like this. "He was never a hoarder, he always said he was a minimalist." I don't know if I believe her.

It is filled knee-deep with clothes and boxes and papers. There is clumping black mould on all the walls. There are two hanging light fixtures, all bulbs broken and still in their sockets. The fridge and stove are unplugged and filled with musty clothes. The only actual carpet I can see amongst the mess is a short path from the blood and fluid-stained spot where his body was found to where the toilet is. His last days were probably a crawl between the two.

This dense, smelly, dark cloistered world is the worst place I have ever been in my life. I would love to erase it but I cannot.

Wondering what she was going to do with her favourite child's ashes upon our return, I was pleased by my mother's response. Louis is to be buried in Memorial Gardens, the bland, any-denominational cemetery on the outskirts of Regina, adjacent to the parking lot of a big box home improvement store.

In her novel 'Claudia,' former Regina resident, Britt Holmström, describes this flat cemetery as:

> ... such a bleak place, that cemetery, frostily forbidding in winter, so unwelcoming you would think the dead are anti-social, a place not designed for meaningful reflection.

Knowing Louis was never religious as an adult, this sounds perfect. What shocks me is Mom's announcement that she has bought four plots: one for Louis, one for Yvette, one for Ape, and one for herself.

Misinterpreting the horrified look on my face, she reminds me I had told her to never buy a cemetery plot as I am donating my body to the Medical School. Not having my own plot is exactly what I want; what I am shocked about is my mother not wanting to be buried in the Catholic cemetery in her hometown of Ponteix, alongside her mother, father, sisters, brother, and every other ancestor since arriving on the prairies a hundred years ago.

Choosing to be the first person of her generation and every previous generation of our Catholic family to not be buried in consecrated ground must have been a momentous decision for her. Her calm statement of where she wants to be buried is so profound, I do not question her decision. I now greatly regret not asking her.

Staring down at the urn of Louis on the floor of her house, Mom and I have a simultaneous thought. Not wanting to say directly what we want, we both skirt around with odd questions like, "I wonder what ashes look like."

I am curious, but know my religious mother will not want to desecrate the urn. Before we left the Vancouver funeral home, we were instructed on how to flip the urn over and unscrew the bottom — just in case airport security wants to open the urn.

With this knowledge, Mom is the first to say, "Let's open it up." It is crazy to say so, but we eagerly open it like two wired kids. Pulling off the bottom, a heavy thick plastic bag plops out, closed with a coiled, metal ring. We bend it open with pliers and sink our hands into the grey ash and gravel, surprised by shards of what feels like egg shells.

We feel great: it is much more hard and crunchy and organic and real than we had ever imagined.

The funeral of St. Louis is a simple affair, and takes place in the beautiful little chapel of Wascana Hospital, so chosen so my sister can be wheeled in from her room for the event.

A female chaplain—same age as me and actually a student of my mom forty years previous—performs the funeral service. It is obviously not a real Mass as women are not allowed to do that. "No chicks at the Last Supper," a classmate once reasoned.

During the brief service, I read a Bible verse my mother has chosen, the chaplain pontificates on God and Jesus Christ and heaven — everything we know Louis stopped believing in when he left high school. I think it is wonderful as the service pleases my mother so much. Funerals are never for the dead.

In my mother's archives, there is a letter from Louis where he sadly apologizes why he cannot lie to her by saying he believes in God, even though he knows doing so will make her so very happy and peaceful. He ends the letter with:

> Everything pales in significance to finding some personal moral code - either religion or just a code of ethics. I shall have to find out which. I really hope the former but will never lie to myself about it. If it's not there, it's not there.

She replies with:

> When I read your letter I felt that my prayers were finally answered. Hope your books will

help you rediscover your faith in a Supreme Being. I will always pray for you, Louis.

Before my big brother's funeral, Mom asks me if I will re-join the Church. I am a coward and do not follow Louis' lead with the blunt truth, instead mumbling my Catholic faith is "on pause" at the moment, whatever the hell that means. My faith and belief are not paused: both have never existed, not even for a moment.

I find a printed email that Louis had sent to our mother:

I just regard death as a stage onto the next stage of awareness, so that is my religion. I have had too many out of the ordinary experiences not to believe that there is no awareness after death, so in a way I look forward to finding out. We have to fully participate in our life experiences for they are there for a reason.

Chapter 50: Laughing With My Sister

In June 1973, at only twenty-one, Yvette receives a professional contract to become part of the medical staff at The Neuro, the famous Montreal Neurological Institute and Hospital (L'Institut et hôpital neurologiques de Montréal.) We are so sad she is leaving but it feels good to see her so excited. This is an early and prestigious boost to her nursing career that she has studied so hard to achieve.

Five months later, she sends a letter to our mother:
> I can no longer adjust nor professionally accept the injustices of ill-health. All we get here is unfortunate car accident victims paralyzed for life, existing on machines. The only thought that prevails is the wish to be left to die. And then the medical gods doing their scientific miracles to preserve a rut existence. Being indoctrinated as a Roman Catholic, I am losing or may unfortunately have lost all belief in a right and just omnipresence. Why must individuals endure such suffering?

She quits her job and returns to Regina by Christmas which makes me so happy. She takes a short mental break here at home, ending with the decision to resume her nursing career. The next sixteen years sees her get married, have two children, start taking a business course, and in 1989, age 37, disappear after a massive brain aneurysm.

For all the time between then and when her body dies, she is stuck halfway between life and death: slightly beyond our grasp of communication, slightly away from the tug of death.

Of the hundreds of times I visit her in Wascana Hospital in Regina and she looks back blankly at me, I feel I am made of paper. I am guessing a religious person would yell and blame God for this never-ending sadistic situation; though terribly sad, not believing in God makes me calm.

In 2008, Yvette's body finally gives up after being in its persistent vegetative state for nearly twenty years. The morning she dies, our mother phones me in a robotic voice:

"David, Yvette has died."

She does not even allow me a moment to absorb this news before finishing with, "I've now lost half my children."

I am so glad my wife and I had moved back to Regina two years previous. Being able to race over to Mom's house at that very moment is an immensely important event in my life.

Once there, I see her in a trance, asking where her other son is. I repeatedly phone Ape, and when he finally answers, I inform him of our sister's death and that we are on our way to the hospital. He says he can't make it there today.

Mom and I arrive at Yvette's room at the long-term care hospital and see a hand-written note on the door: "Do Not Enter. Family Only."

I am frozen in terror. If Mom was not beside me, I may never have opened that door. I do, we enter and see Yvette the most peaceful ever. She is lying on her back, eyes closed, her upper lip on one side slightly upturned — in a sort of smirk.

The Head Nurse arrives, offers her condolences, and asks my mother to come with her to the front desk to fill out all the appropriate paperwork. This leaves me alone with my dead sister.

Mom leaves, ordering me to gather Yvette's possessions. Out of nervousness or simply not knowing how to react, I start talking out loud non-stop to my sister as I fill boxes with clothes and photos and blankets. Many wonderful stories fill my head. I am babbling in a hilarious monologue; Yvette lies there grinning.

I have always had visions of her bright eyes popping open, her toothy grin appearing, "Ha! Fooled you guys!" and her big ta-dah bow. Today, for the first time, holding her cold hands, I realize it is not going to happen.

Mom is gone for a long time and when she arrives back, she is startled to see me sitting by Yvette's side, laughing — my shirt damp with tears.

My sister's body is cremated in December, its ashes stored in an urn at Memorial Gardens until we can arrange a funeral on a warm day sometime the next spring. No one wants to attend a freezing cold, windy, winter funeral in Saskatchewan.

Mom and I start to make plans for Yvette's service to be in the same hospital chapel as her big brother's, to have the same female chaplain, and to have the same Bible readings. We pride ourselves on our great organizational skills, though she messes up all our plans by dying too.

Chapter 51: A Beautiful Death

Mom goes away with her rubber boots on. Her greatest personal pleasure in life is always being in her vegetable garden and that is where she spends her last afternoon.

She has a massive brain attack and her body plops down in her beautiful garden, amongst her award-winning carrots (the sweetest, most delicious carrots I will ever eat), her insect friends fluttering about. Sad as it is, having your elderly mother die is a natural part of life, made even more poignant when it's a beautiful death. Dying in her garden, after a day in the fresh air, is exactly what she would have wanted.

Though her brain explodes and "Mom" is gone before her body hits the ground, her body does not actually die there and then. It is in a coma in Intensive Care for a few days, in a room filled with machines keeping it alive —everything she does not want. Many years prior, she asks me to be her legal guardian in this hypothetical situation and I deliver a copy of her Personal Directive to the doctors and nurses who are all impressed. This is the most detailed directive they have ever read.

I am shocked to see Ape arrive, usually absent for everything family related. Together we listen to the doctor describe the massive brain damage, that there is zero probability of any sort of conscious recovery, that her Personal Directive is clear, and asks us to sign off on "pulling the plug."

As her Legal Guardian, I grab a pen, and reach over—

"For fuck sakes! She'll be fine!" Ape startles us. "Mom's

tough as nails. She'll be in her garden next week." We stare at Ape, completely dumbfounded.

The dazed doctor looks back at me, expecting me to say something. I shrug. He reluctantly schedules another family meeting two days hence.

That time span is hell for me and I do not sleep a wink. I cannot help thinking that I am going to look like the bad guy in Ape's eyes: I am the one who will say to pull the plug, I am the one who will kill our mother. I know if Ape does not agree to remove the life support in the next meeting that I, the little brother, the person our mother has chosen to be her Legal Guardian, will have to pull rank and overrule any objection.

I do not see Ape for those two tumultuous days as he never visits his dying mother's body. He does surprisingly show up for the big meeting. The doctor once again presents the same prognosis. Ape remains silent. I do not know why. I sign the papers, we walk over to our mother's huge room filled with machines, and wait in the hallway as the nurses disengage the breathing tube.

In a Hollywood movie, the two sons would sadly slowly enter the room, sit on either side of the bed, each softly holding one hand of their mother as she takes her final calm breath, cry a tear, then stand up to give each other a powerful loud hug — one they have waited their entire lives to give one another.

That did not happen in our reality.

Mom is lying quite peaceful, breathing on her own, with Ape and I standing on either side of the bed.

After a few moments, he grunts "Gotta go!"

As he leaves, I spread my arms as does he. My wife later describes it as the most awkward, non-emotional hug she has ever seen in her life.

(During school dances in the 1970s, the Nuns were always vigilant during soft ballads, making sure there was always 'room for the Holy Spirit' between the boy and girl dancers. When Ape and I hugged our first/only/final hug, the entire two-thousand year Catechism could easily have fit between us.)

My comatose mother's body is transferred to a hospice, one with ten palliative care private rooms each named after a Canadian province. Serendipity has her in the Québec room; coincidence has her in the same room and bed where her only brother died a few years prior. There, late on a Sunday evening, less than a week after her brain seizure, when I alone hold her hand, her breathing gets shallower and shallower and simply silently stops at midnight.

I am in a soft daze, holding her hand for quite awhile when I'm surprised to hear my own voice whispering, "Thank you ... thank you ... thank you ..."

The first phone call I make, of course, is to my brother. A woman answers. I say who I am and it is important I talk to my brother right now. She says he is asleep and there is no way she can wake him. I say I must talk to him, that our mother died a few minutes ago.

"He's gotta fucken work tomorrow," she says, and hangs up.

199

Chapter 52: Dying Stupid

I myself do not care when I die. It is how I die which bothers me. I do not want to die stupid. I want people crying at my funeral, not muffling giggles.

One morning when I was 33 —same age as Christ when he died— I step out of the shower as I've done thousands of times before. (Nothing fancy or dramatic — no stripper twirl on the shower curtain.) Simply stepping out of the tub and BAM!: an intensely sharp pain in my right side, forcing me drop to the bathmat, holding my side in agony. I have no idea how but I must have twisted a muscle in my back or side.

In pain and with laboured breathing for a day, I finally accept it's not going away, so I walk the dozen blocks to the hospital where I get a chest x-ray.

The doctor returns to my examining room, flips the x-ray film up on the light box, leans in, and squeals, "Oh my God!" and races out of the room. All I see is his white coat flash by me and the door close. Absolutely the worst bedside manner I've ever seen.

Two nurses run in and tell me they will start prepping me for lung surgery. Seems I've had a spontaneous pneumothorax: my right lung has torn away from the chest wall and has half-collapsed. Emergency surgery is needed immediately as the lung will continue to collapse, taking the other lung with it.

If I had died there in E.R. or during surgery, everyone I

know would have been so saddened with the news. That is, until they ask a few questions.

"Did David fall in the tub and smash his chest?"

"Well … no …"

"Something hit him and crushed his lung?"

"Well … no …"

"Well, what happened?"

"He, ah, he just stepped out of the shower."

"And?"

"That's it."

"What? He steps out of the shower, tears a lung, and dies?"

"Yup."

"Oh geez, what a dork."

If I am dead when you read this and you know I died in an embarrassingly stupid manner, please ignore that and force yourself to cry at my funeral — pinching yourself if need be.

PART SIX: HEAVEN

Chapter 53: Heaven

I do not know if Ape is still alive. I assume he is, though I have no idea who would tell me if he was gone. We have not seen each other since he popped into our mother's funeral in 2009 — and we will never see each other again, neither going to the funeral of whoever dies first. Away from writing this book, he never crosses my mind. I am sure he is still around, most likely in a small town somewhere, always on the lookout for the "god-damn cops."

"There's your Mom!" I yelp to my two nieces on Canada Day a few years ago. We are strolling through a park in Kelowna during the holiday celebrations when I see Yvette's current-day doppelgänger amongst a large drum circle of old, grey-haired hippies. She is wild dancing barefoot by herself on the grass, with the biggest, most beautiful smile in the world. I am hoping my nieces do not see my eyes filled with tears as we walk by.

My sister's two daughters are doing quite well in prestigious positions: one in medicine, the other in computer systems. They lost their mother at ages eleven and eight, with Yvette leaving them before getting a chance to clarify and correct her many wild stories. That task was left with me.

As for me, now, in my late fifties, I think I am doing extremely well. I own my own business, happily married for twenty-five years, and have two wonderful puggle dogs.

205

I often wonder why I never for a moment had the thrill of receiving the divine spark, though I have always been fully open for it. My first decade of life was an unsuccessful indoctrination into the Roman Catholic Church and I have no idea why it was a complete failure: I was the perfect candidate in the most fertile environment. Why did God make me an atheist?

As I have had quite a bit of experience in writing obituaries, I thought it best if I end this book with my own. (My survivors can do a final polish before publication.)

LOBLAW David Robert. 1960-20[xx]

David tragically passed away last week when he was struck by a [meteorite / bus / llama]. David is pleased his final words of "What the —" will be etched into the pedestal of the thirty-foot marble statue his wife will build for his memorial monument. Upon showing his Holy Card, David was allowed into Heaven and warmly hugged by his incredulous mother, sister, brother, and father. As they bring him back to their table, David notices Leonard Cohen singing on stage. They nod to each other. Yapping and twirling around David's feet are all of his long-lost cats and dogs, plus the rabbit he killed for Grade 11 Biology. Together in an aquarium are his pet turtles and award-winning planarians. "Soup's on!" his mother announces, opening the lid to a giant pot of chicken noodle soup. Yvette and Louis sit beside each other, laughing; Alfred is next to Irene, holding her hand. As David sits, his sister places Ricky on his lap.

ABOUT THE AUTHOR

David Robert Loblaw lives on the windy flatlands of Canada with his wife and hound dogs. He has never learned to type with more than one finger or swim.

His lifelong dream of becoming an astronaut will start to come true this weekend when he wins the big lottery.

See photos and videos of his hometown at drloblaw.com

Made in the USA
San Bernardino, CA
10 December 2018